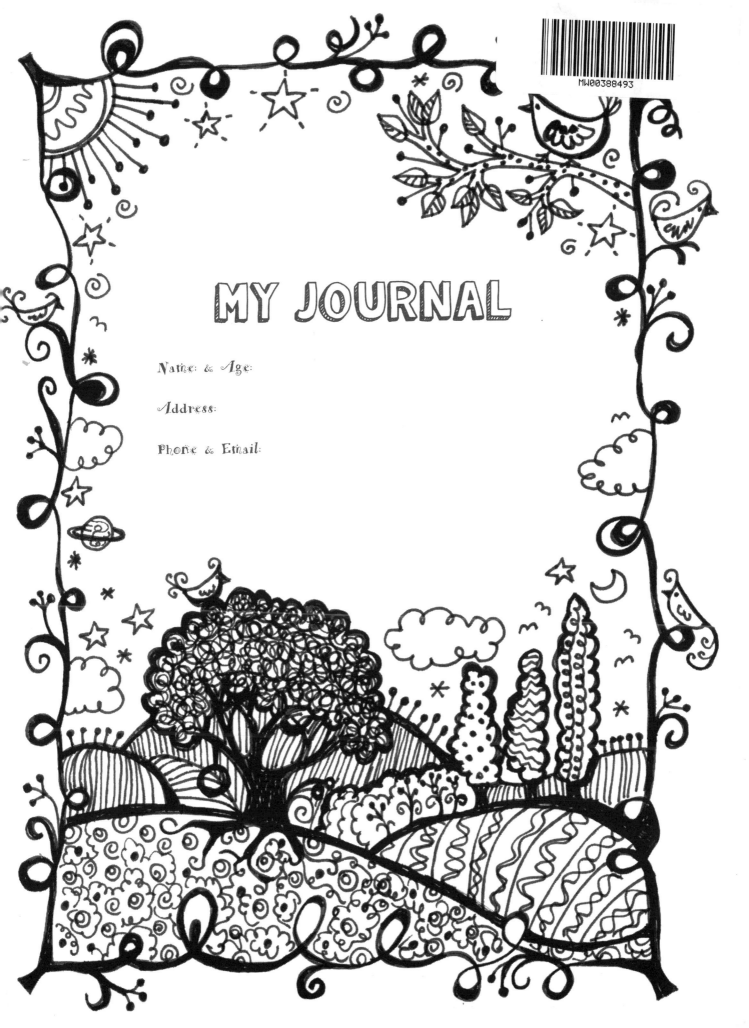

MY JOURNAL

Name: & Age:

Address:

Phone & Email:

Do It Yourself
HOMESCHOOL
JOURNALS

Copyright Information

Contact Us:

The Thinking Tree LLC
617 N. Swope St. Greenfield, IN 46140. United States
317.622.8852 PHONE (Dial +1 outside of the USA) 267.712.7889 FAX
www.DyslexiaGames.com
jbrown@DyslexiaGames.com

INSTRUCTIONS

LIST or DRAW NINE THINGS
That you want to learn about:

1.
2.
3.
4.
5.
6.
7.
8.
9.

Action Steps:

1. Go to the library or bookstore.
2. Bring home a stack of at least NINE interesting books about these topics. Choose some that have diagrams, instructions and illustrations.

Supplies Needed:

You will need pencils, colored pencils, pens and markers.

Choose Nine Books To Use As School Books!

1. Write down the titles on each cover below.
2. Keep your stack of book in a safe place.
3. Be ready to read a few pages from your books daily.
4. Complete 10 pages each day in this workbook.

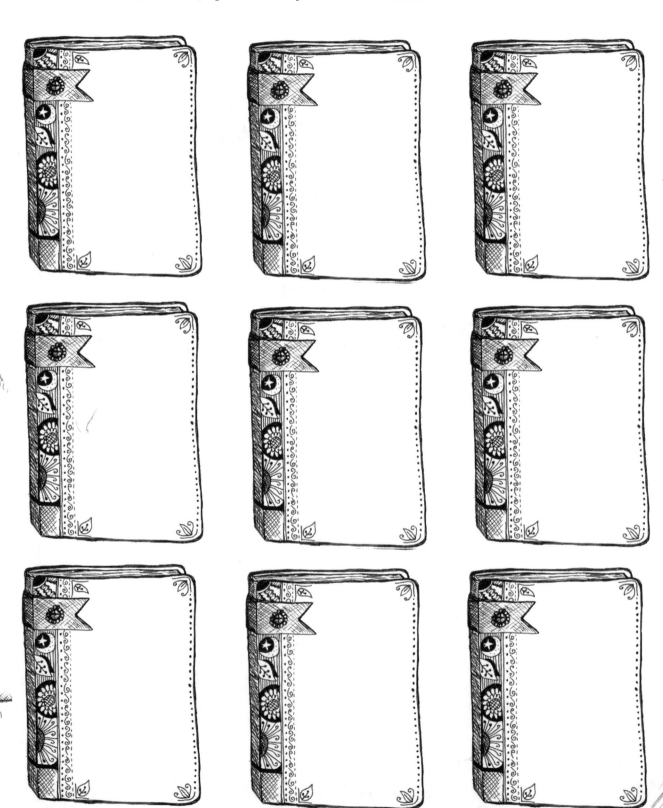

Circle Today's Date

January
February
March
April
May
June
July
August
September
October
November
December

1 2 3 4 5 6
7 8 9 10 11
12 13 14 15
16 17 18 19
20 21 22 23
24 25 26 27
28 29 30 31

MONDAY
TUESDAY
WEDNESDAY
THURSDAY
FRIDAY
SATURDAY
SUNDAY

2015
2016
2017
2018
2019
2020
2021
2023
2024
2025
2026
2027
2028
2029
2030

Write Today's Date:_____

Start Your Day!

Inspirational Verse or Quote

_____
_____
_____
_____
_____
_____

Prayer Needs

_____
_____
_____

To-Do List

_____
_____
_____
_____

Art & Logic Games

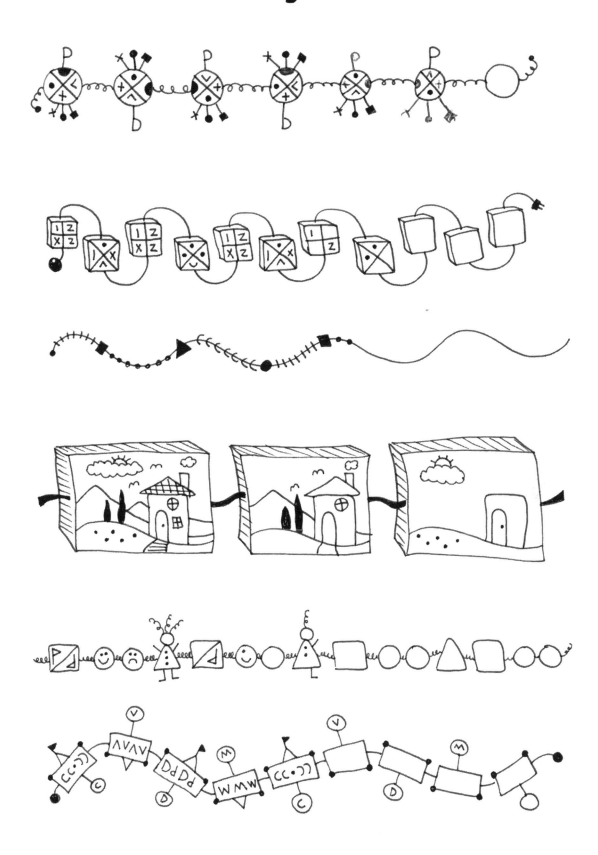

Nature Study

Go outside and make a realistic drawing of something you find in in nature.

Reading Time

Read a few pages from four books in your stack.

Copy something from each book.

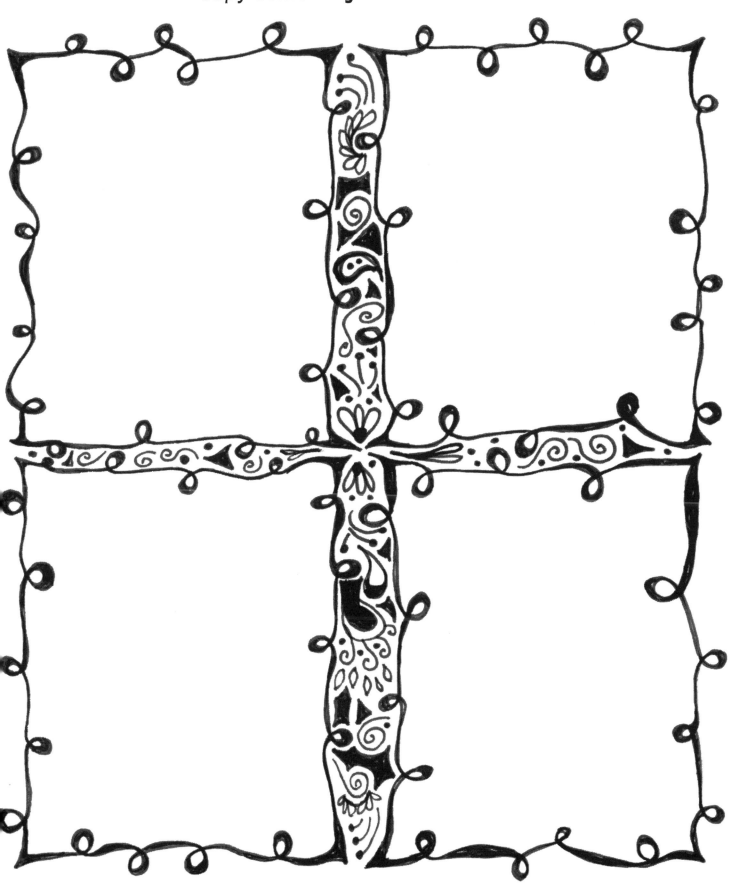

Spelling Time

Find 20 Words with 4 letters each.
Write the words here:

Start Time:

_ _ _ _ _

Stop Time:

_ _ _ _ _

Screen Time!

Watch a Documentary, Educational Program, Movie, or Tutorial.

TITLE: _____

SUBJECT _____

LOCATION: _____

YEAR: _____

MESSAGE: _____

Rating:

AWFUL

BAD

LAME

YUCKY

OKAY

NICE

GOOD

GREAT

SUPER

AMAZING

Draw a Scene from the video:

Notes:

TITLE:

World News Today!

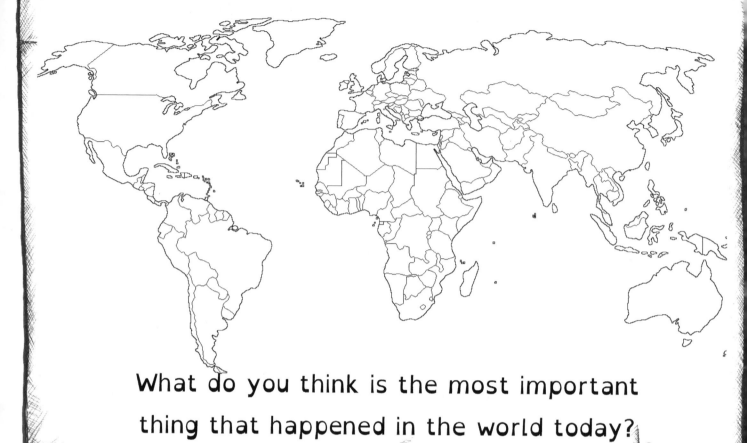

What do you think is the most important thing that happened in the world today?

Tell the story with words or pictures.

Writing Time

Stories, Poems, Lists and More.
That's what this page is waiting for!

_____

_____

_____

_____

_____

_____

_____

_____

_____

_____

_____

_____

_____

_____

_____

_____

_____

_____

_____

Circle Today's Date

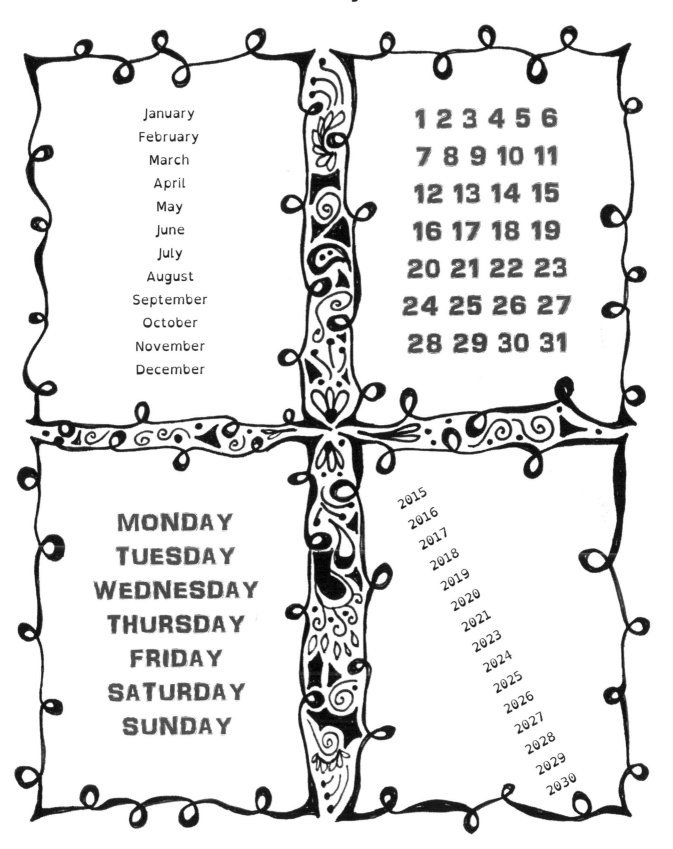

January
February
March
April
May
June
July
August
September
October
November
December

1 2 3 4 5 6
7 8 9 10 11
12 13 14 15
16 17 18 19
20 21 22 23
24 25 26 27
28 29 30 31

MONDAY
TUESDAY
WEDNESDAY
THURSDAY
FRIDAY
SATURDAY
SUNDAY

2015
2016
2017
2018
2019
2020
2021
2023
2024
2025
2026
2027
2028
2029
2030

Write Today's Date:_____

Start Your Day!

Inspirational Verse or Quote

_____

_____

_____

_____

_____

_____

Prayer Needs

_____

_____

_____

_____

To-Do List

_____

_____

_____

_____

_____

_____

Art & Logic Games

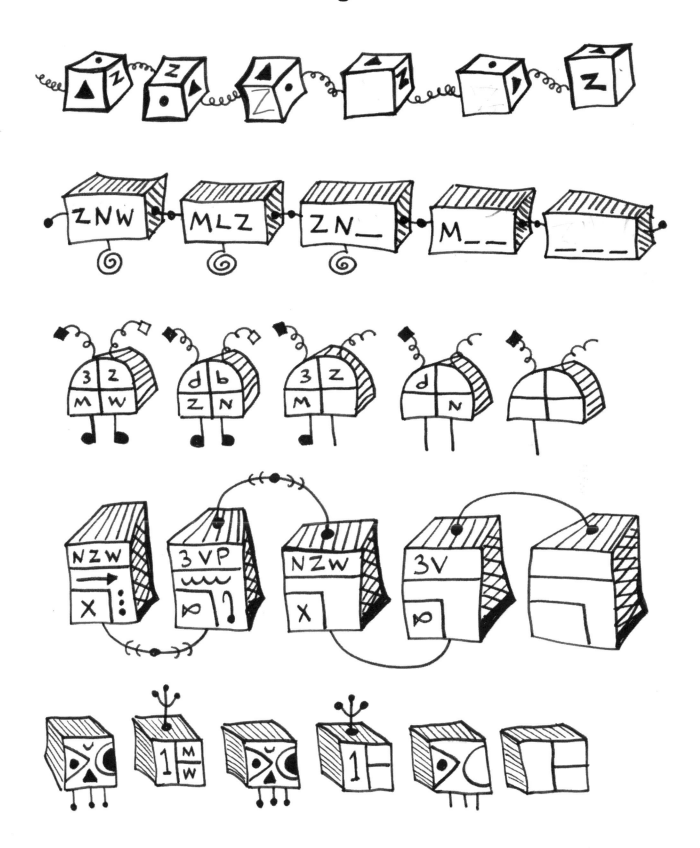

Nature Study

Go outside and make a realistic drawing of something you find in in nature.

Reading Time

Read a few pages from four books in your stack.

Copy something from each book.

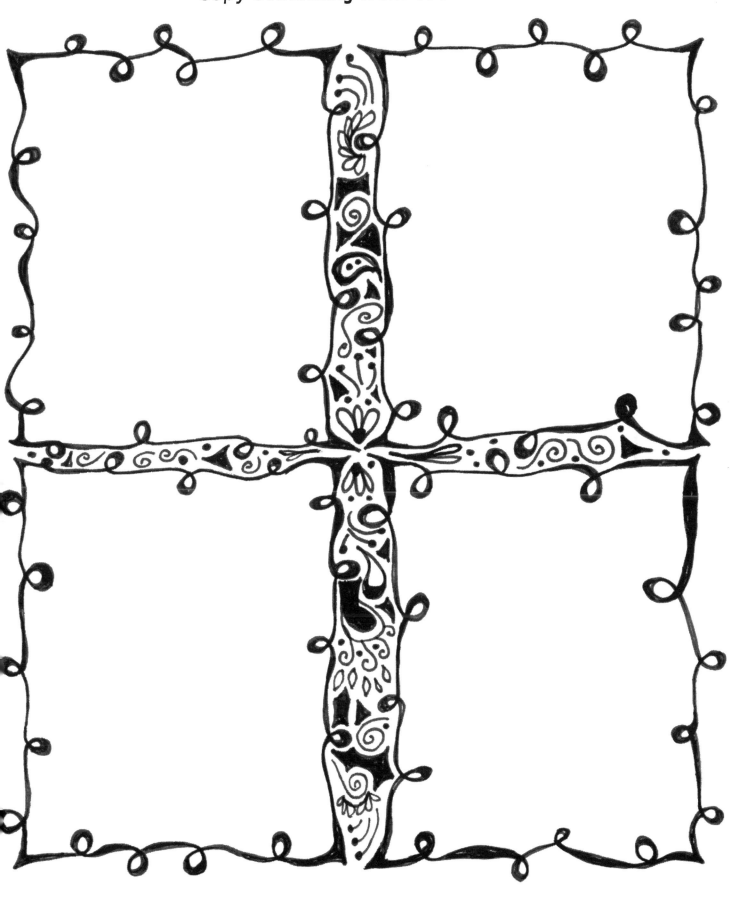

Spelling Time

Find 20 Words with 5 letters each.
Write the words here:

_____   _____

_____   _____

_____   _____

_____   _____

_____   _____

_____   _____

_____   _____

_____   _____

_____   _____

_____   _____

Screen Time!
Watch a Documentary, Educational Program, Movie, or Tutorial.

Start Time:
_____

Stop Time:
_____

TITLE: _____

SUBJECT _____

LOCATION: _____

YEAR: _____

MESSAGE: _____

Rating:
AWFUL
BAD
LAME
YUCKY
OKAY
NICE
GOOD
GREAT
SUPER
AMAZING

Draw a Scene from the video:

Notes:

TITLE:

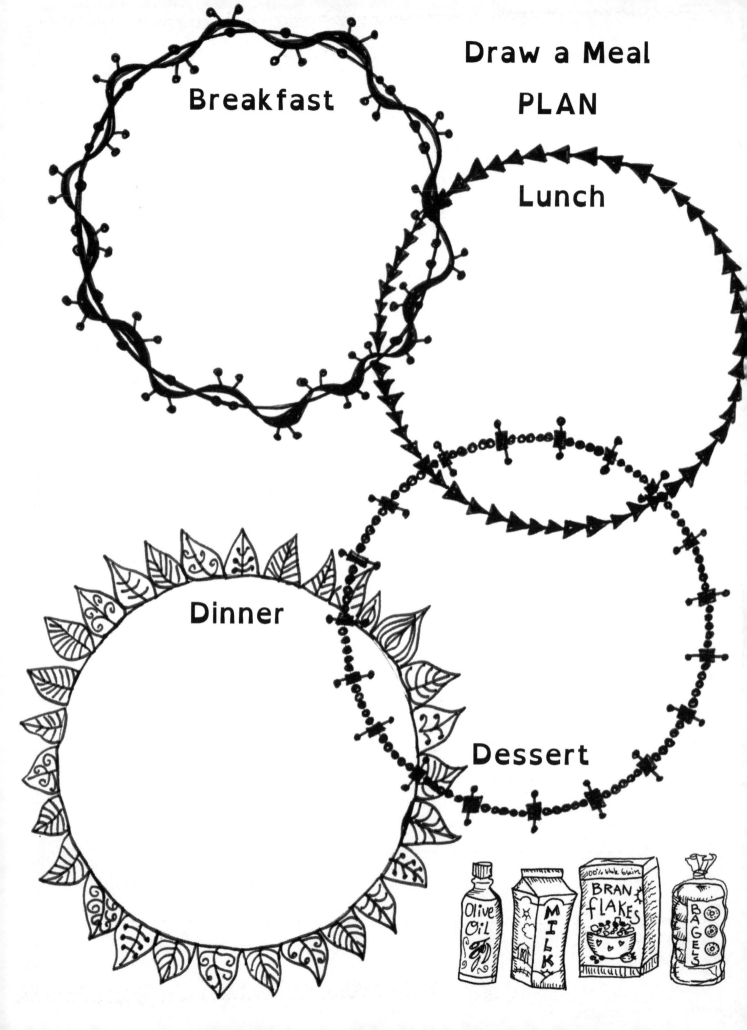

Writing Time

Stories, Poems, Lists and More.
That's what this page is waiting for!

_____

_____

_____

_____

_____

_____

_____

_____

_____

_____

_____

_____

_____

_____

_____

_____

_____

_____

Circle Today's Date

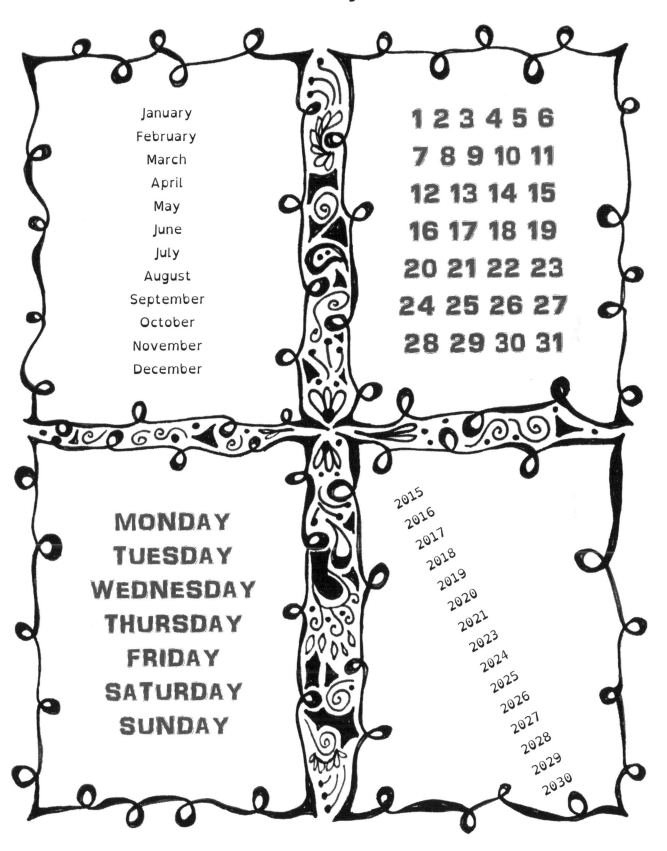

January
February
March
April
May
June
July
August
September
October
November
December

1 2 3 4 5 6
7 8 9 10 11
12 13 14 15
16 17 18 19
20 21 22 23
24 25 26 27
28 29 30 31

MONDAY
TUESDAY
WEDNESDAY
THURSDAY
FRIDAY
SATURDAY
SUNDAY

2015
2016
2017
2018
2019
2020
2021
2023
2024
2025
2026
2027
2028
2029
2030

Write Today's Date:_____

Start Your Day!

Inspirational Verse or Quote

_____

_____

_____

_____

_____

_____

Prayer Needs

_____

_____

_____

To-Do List

_____

_____

_____

_____

_____

Art & Logic Games

Nature Study

Go outside and make a realistic drawing of something you find in in nature.

Reading Time

Read a few pages from four books in your stack.

Copy something from each book.

Spelling Time

Find 20 Words with 6 letters each.
Write the words here:

_____   _____

_____   _____

_____   _____

_____   _____

_____   _____

_____   _____

_____   _____

_____   _____

_____   _____

_____   _____

Start Time:

_ _ _ _ _

Stop Time:

_ _ _ _ _

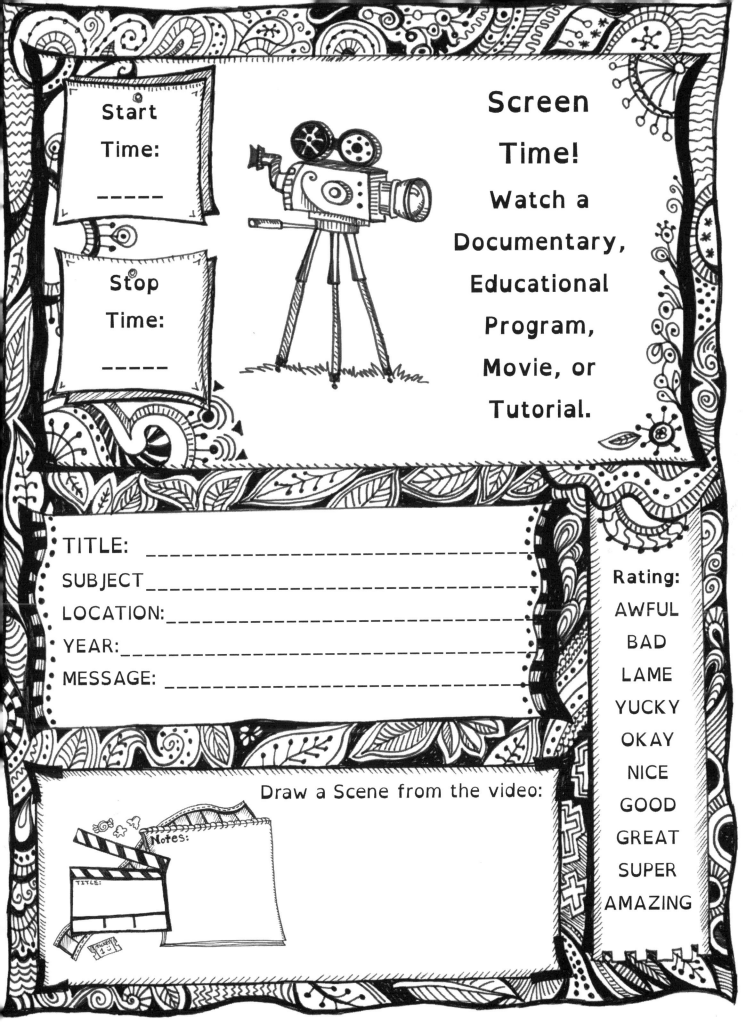

Screen Time!

Watch a Documentary, Educational Program, Movie, or Tutorial.

TITLE: _____

SUBJECT _____

LOCATION: _____

YEAR: _____

MESSAGE: _____

Rating:

AWFUL

BAD

LAME

YUCKY

OKAY

NICE

GOOD

GREAT

SUPER

AMAZING

Draw a Scene from the video:

Notes:

TITLE:

DRAW THE PAST, PRESENT & FUTURE

Of _____

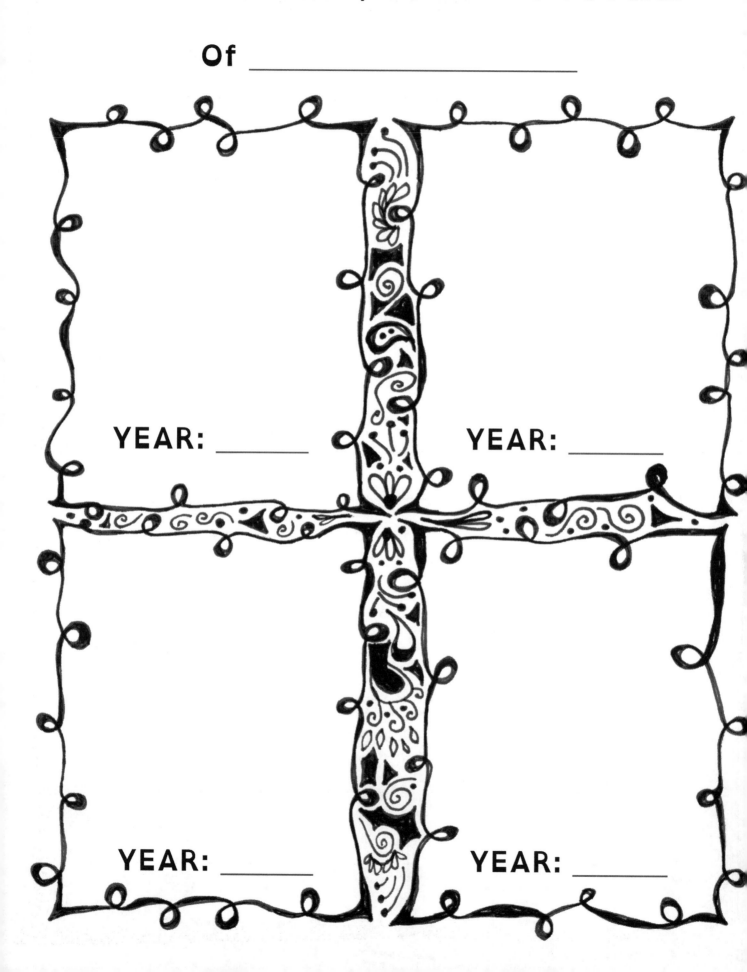

YEAR: _____

YEAR: _____

YEAR: _____

YEAR: _____

Writing Time

Stories, Poems, Lists and More.
That's what this page is waiting for!

_____

_____

_____

_____

_____

_____

_____

_____

_____

_____

_____

_____

_____

_____

_____

_____

_____

Circle Today's Date

January
February
March
April
May
June
July
August
September
October
November
December

1 2 3 4 5 6
7 8 9 10 11
12 13 14 15
16 17 18 19
20 21 22 23
24 25 26 27
28 29 30 31

MONDAY
TUESDAY
WEDNESDAY
THURSDAY
FRIDAY
SATURDAY
SUNDAY

2015
2016
2017
2018
2019
2020
2021
2023
2024
2025
2026
2027
2028
2029
2030

Write Today's Date:_____

Start Your Day!

Inspirational Verse or Quote

_____

_____

_____

_____

_____

_____

Prayer Needs

_____

_____

_____

_____

To-Do List

_____

_____

_____

_____

_____

Art & Logic Games

Nature Study

Go outside and make a realistic
drawing of something you find in
in nature.

Reading Time

Read a few pages from four books in your stack.

Copy something from each book.

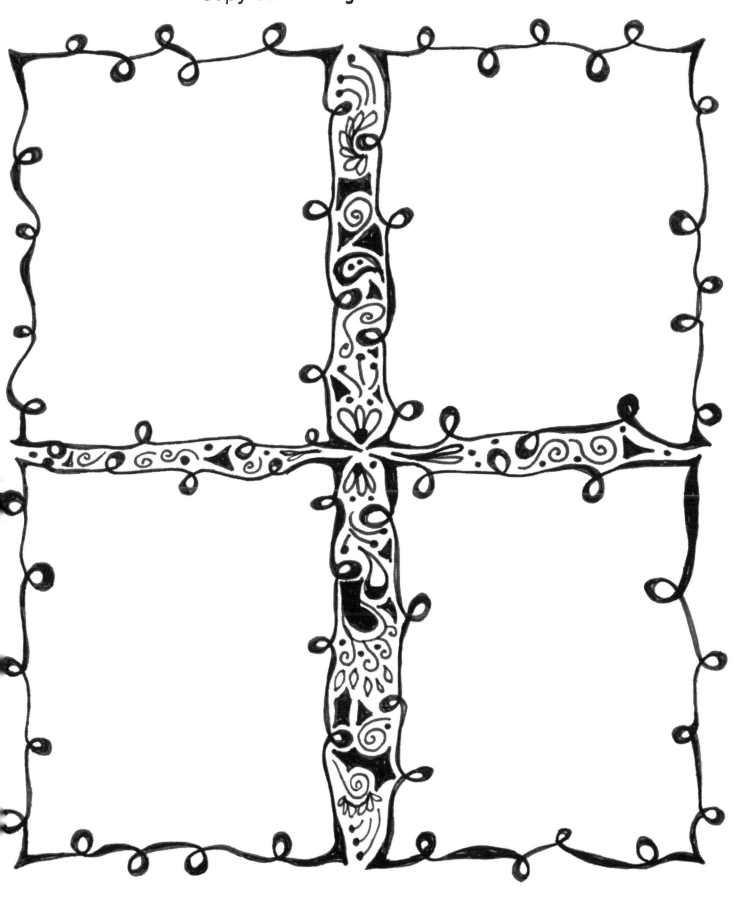

Spelling Time

Find 20 Words with **7** letters each.
Write the words here:

_____   _____

_____   _____

_____   _____

_____   _____

_____   _____

_____   _____

_____   _____

_____   _____

_____   _____

_____   _____

Start Time: _ _ _ _ _

Stop Time: _ _ _ _ _

Screen Time!

Watch a Documentary, Educational Program, Movie, or Tutorial.

TITLE: _____

SUBJECT_____

LOCATION:_____

YEAR:_____

MESSAGE: _____

Rating:

AWFUL

BAD

LAME

YUCKY

OKAY

NICE

GOOD

GREAT

SUPER

AMAZING

Draw a Scene from the video:

Notes:

TITLE:

Writing Time

Stories, Poems, Lists and More.
That's what this page is waiting for!

_____

_____

_____

_____

_____

_____

_____

_____

_____

_____

_____

_____

_____

_____

_____

_____

_____

_____

Circle Today's Date

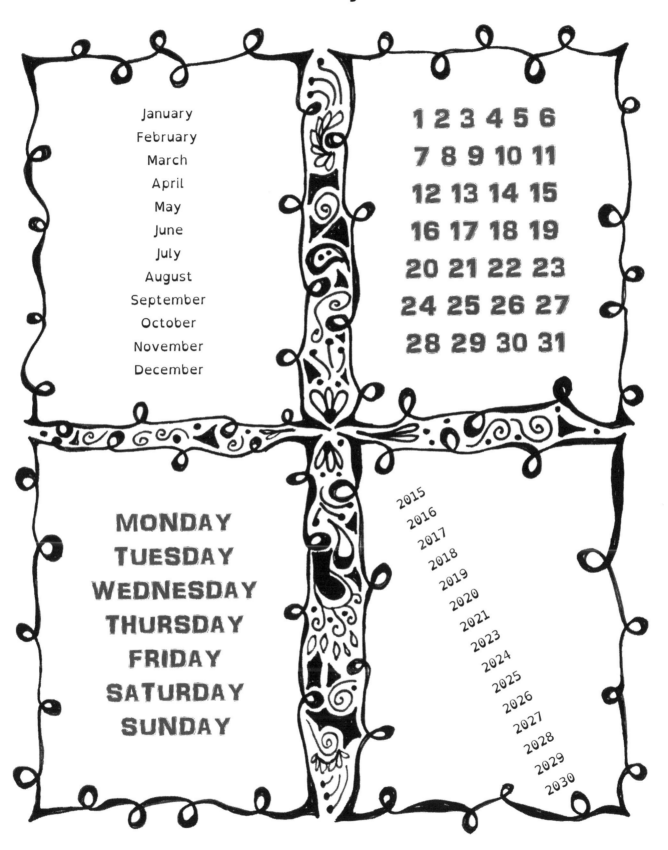

January
February
March
April
May
June
July
August
September
October
November
December

1 2 3 4 5 6
7 8 9 10 11
12 13 14 15
16 17 18 19
20 21 22 23
24 25 26 27
28 29 30 31

MONDAY
TUESDAY
WEDNESDAY
THURSDAY
FRIDAY
SATURDAY
SUNDAY

2015
2016
2017
2018
2019
2020
2021
2023
2024
2025
2026
2027
2028
2029
2030

Write Today's Date:_____

Start Your Day!

Inspirational Verse or Quote

_____

_____

_____

_____

_____

_____

Prayer Needs

_____

_____

_____

_____

To-Do List

_____

_____

_____

_____

_____

_____

_____

Art & Logic Games

Nature Study

Go outside and make a realistic drawing of something you find in in nature.

Reading Time

Read a few pages from four books in your stack.

Copy something from each book.

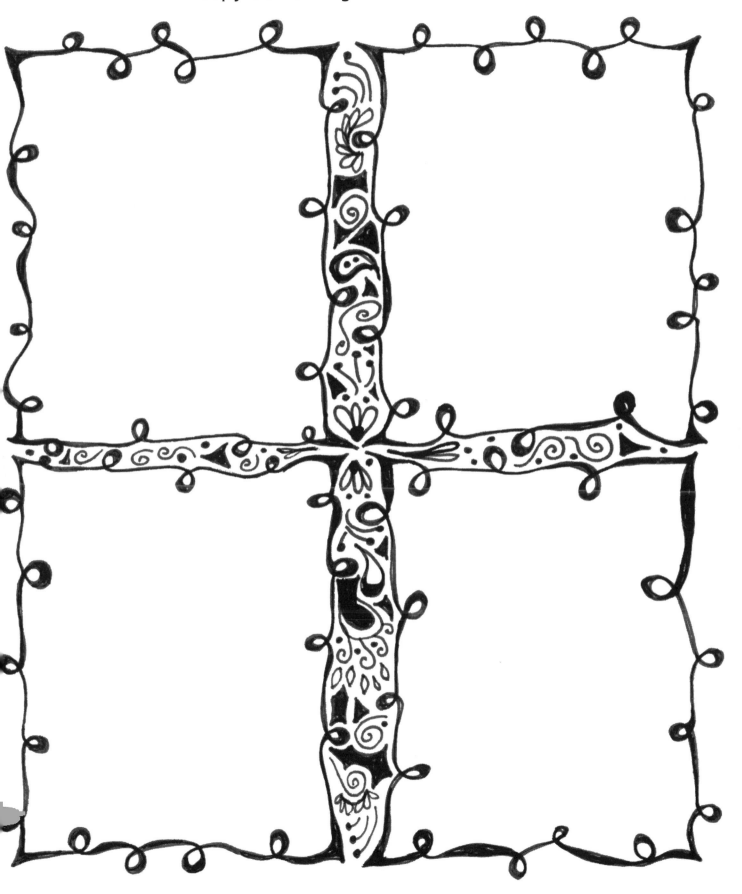

Spelling Time

Find 20 Words with 8 letters each.
Write the words here:

Start Time:

_ _ _ _ _

Stop Time:

_ _ _ _ _

Screen Time!

Watch a Documentary, Educational Program, Movie, or Tutorial.

TITLE: _____

SUBJECT _____

LOCATION:_____

YEAR:_____

MESSAGE: _____

Rating:

AWFUL

BAD

LAME

YUCKY

OKAY

NICE

GOOD

GREAT

SUPER

AMAZING

Notes:

TITLE:

Draw a Scene from the video:

Listening Time

Listen to an audio book or classical music or ask someone to read a story to you while you color and draw on the next page.

What are you listening to?

_____

Circle Today's Date

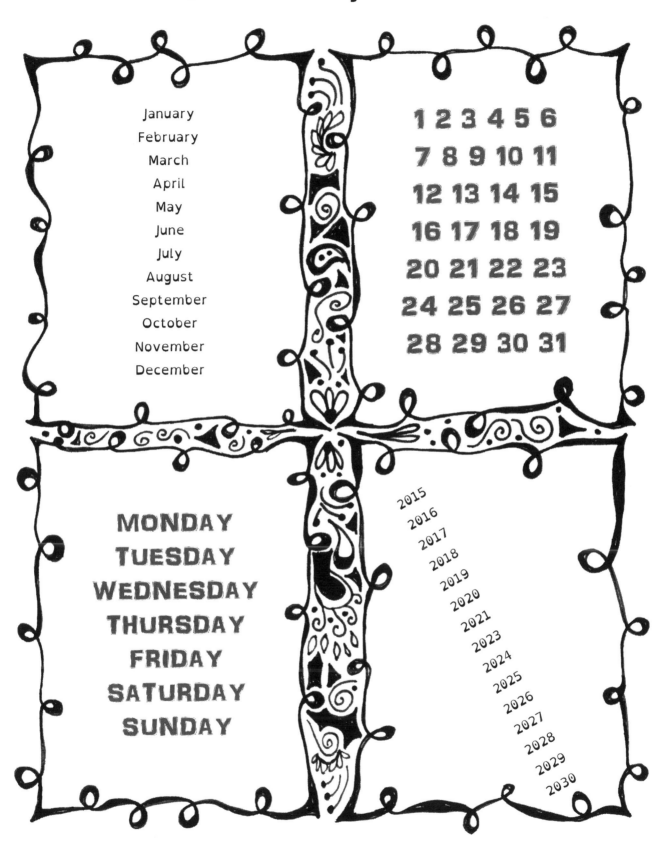

January
February
March
April
May
June
July
August
September
October
November
December

1 2 3 4 5 6
7 8 9 10 11
12 13 14 15
16 17 18 19
20 21 22 23
24 25 26 27
28 29 30 31

MONDAY
TUESDAY
WEDNESDAY
THURSDAY
FRIDAY
SATURDAY
SUNDAY

2015
2016
2017
2018
2019
2020
2021
2023
2024
2025
2026
2027
2028
2029
2030

Write Today's Date:_____

Start Your Day!

Inspirational Verse or Quote

_____

_____

_____

_____

_____

_____

Prayer Needs

_____

_____

_____

To-Do List

_____

_____

_____

_____

_____

Art & Logic Games

Nature Study

Go outside and make a realistic drawing of something you find in in nature.

Reading Time

Read a few pages from four books in your stack.

Copy something from each book.

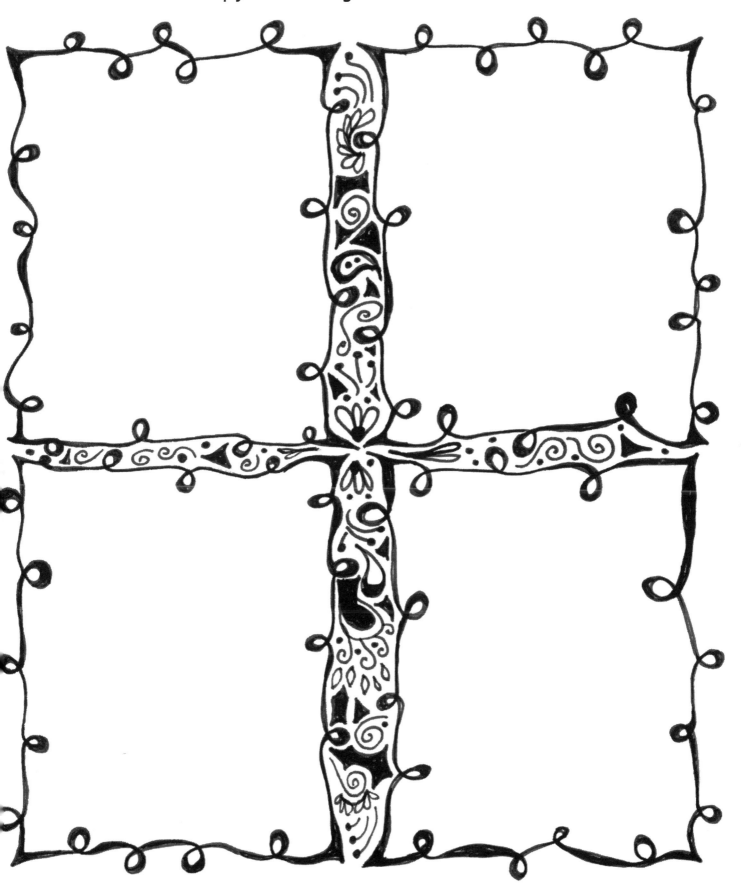

Spelling Time

Find 20 Words with 9 letters each.
Write the words here:

_____   _____

_____   _____

_____   _____

_____   _____

_____   _____

_____   _____

_____   _____

_____   _____

_____   _____

_____   _____

Screen Time!

Watch a Documentary, Educational Program, Movie, or Tutorial.

Start Time:

_____

Stop Time:

_____

TITLE: _____

SUBJECT_____

LOCATION:_____

YEAR:_____

MESSAGE: _____

Rating:

AWFUL

BAD

LAME

YUCKY

OKAY

NICE

GOOD

GREAT

SUPER

AMAZING

Draw a Scene from the video:

Notes:

TITLE:

World News Today!

What do you think is the most important
thing that happened in the world today?

Tell the story with words or pictures.

Writing Time

Stories, Poems, Lists and More.
That's what this page is waiting for!

_____

_____

_____

_____

_____

_____

_____

_____

_____

_____

_____

_____

_____

_____

_____

_____

_____

Circle Today's Date

January
February
March
April
May
June
July
August
September
October
November
December

1 2 3 4 5 6
7 8 9 10 11
12 13 14 15
16 17 18 19
20 21 22 23
24 25 26 27
28 29 30 31

MONDAY
TUESDAY
WEDNESDAY
THURSDAY
FRIDAY
SATURDAY
SUNDAY

2015
2016
2017
2018
2019
2020
2021
2023
2024
2025
2026
2027
2028
2029
2030

Write Today's Date:_____

Start Your Day!

Inspirational Verse or Quote

_____

_____

_____

_____

_____

_____

Prayer Needs

_____

_____

_____

To-Do List

_____

_____

_____

_____

Art & Logic Games

Nature Study

Go outside and make a realistic drawing of something you find in in nature.

Reading Time

Read a few pages from four books in your stack.

Copy something from each book.

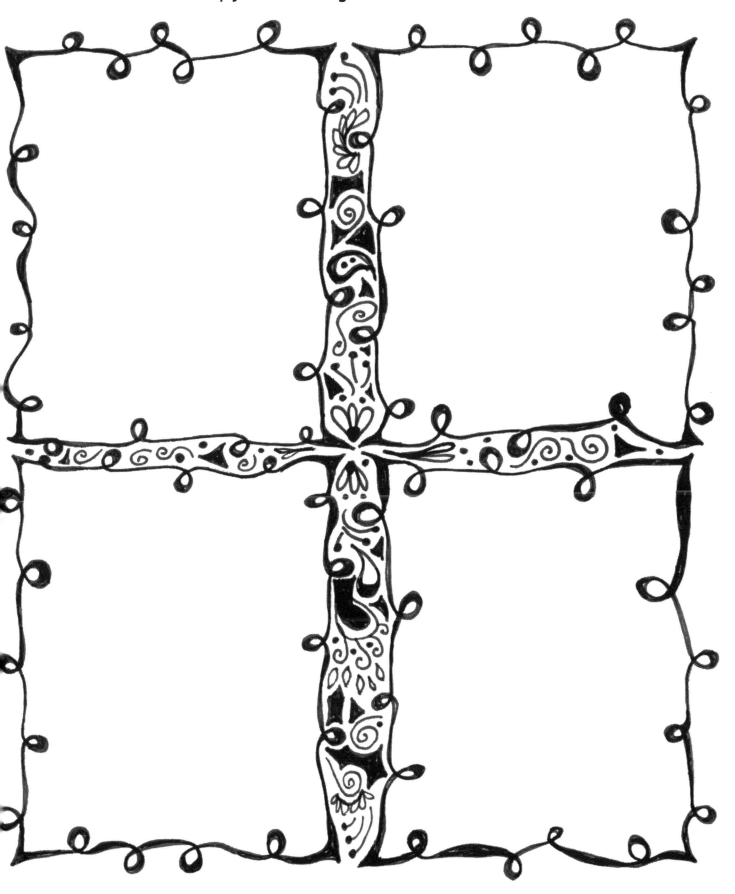

Spelling Time

Find 20 Words with **8** letters each.

Write the words here:

_____   _____

_____   _____

_____   _____

_____   _____

_____   _____

_____   _____

_____   _____

_____   _____

_____   _____

_____   _____

Screen Time!

Start Time:

_ _ _ _ _

Stop Time:

_ _ _ _ _

Watch a Documentary, Educational Program, Movie, or Tutorial.

TITLE: _____

SUBJECT_____

LOCATION:_____

YEAR:_____

MESSAGE: _____

Rating:

AWFUL

BAD

LAME

YUCKY

OKAY

NICE

GOOD

GREAT

SUPER

AMAZING

Draw a Scene from the video:

Notes:

TITLE:

DRAW THE PAST, PRESENT & FUTURE

Of _____

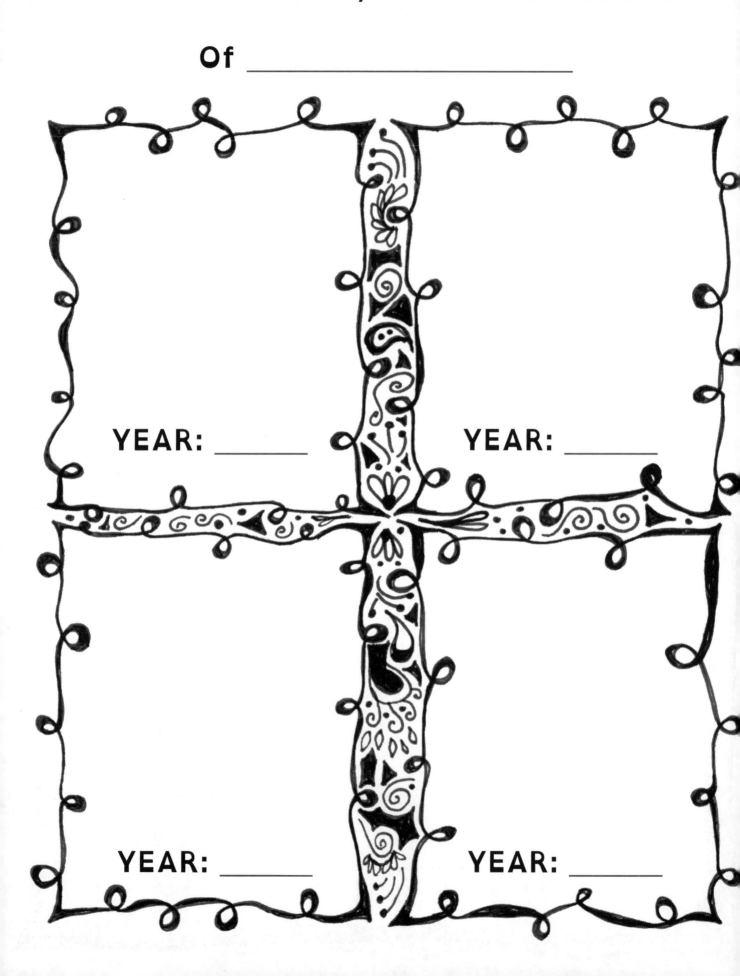

YEAR: _____

YEAR: _____

YEAR: _____

YEAR: _____

Writing Time

Stories, Poems, Lists and More.
That's what this page is waiting for!

_____

_____

_____

_____

_____

_____

_____

_____

_____

_____

_____

_____

_____

_____

_____

_____

_____

_____

_____

Circle Today's Date

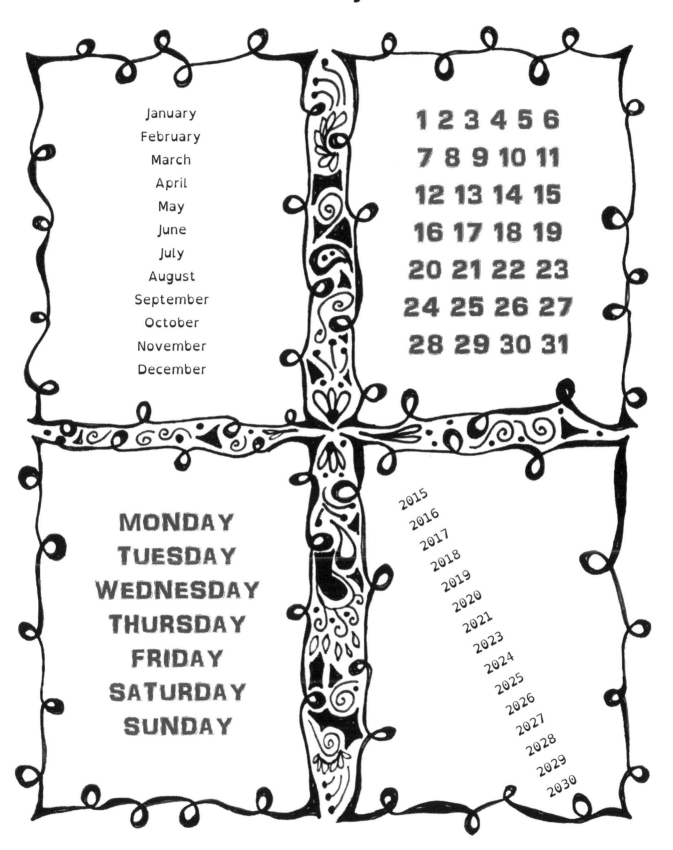

January
February
March
April
May
June
July
August
September
October
November
December

1 2 3 4 5 6
7 8 9 10 11
12 13 14 15
16 17 18 19
20 21 22 23
24 25 26 27
28 29 30 31

MONDAY
TUESDAY
WEDNESDAY
THURSDAY
FRIDAY
SATURDAY
SUNDAY

2015
2016
2017
2018
2019
2020
2021
2023
2024
2025
2026
2027
2028
2029
2030

Write Today's Date:_____

Start Your Day!

Inspirational Verse or Quote

_____
_____
_____
_____
_____
_____

Prayer Needs

_____
_____
_____
_____

To-Do List

_____
_____
_____
_____
_____
_____

Art & Logic Games

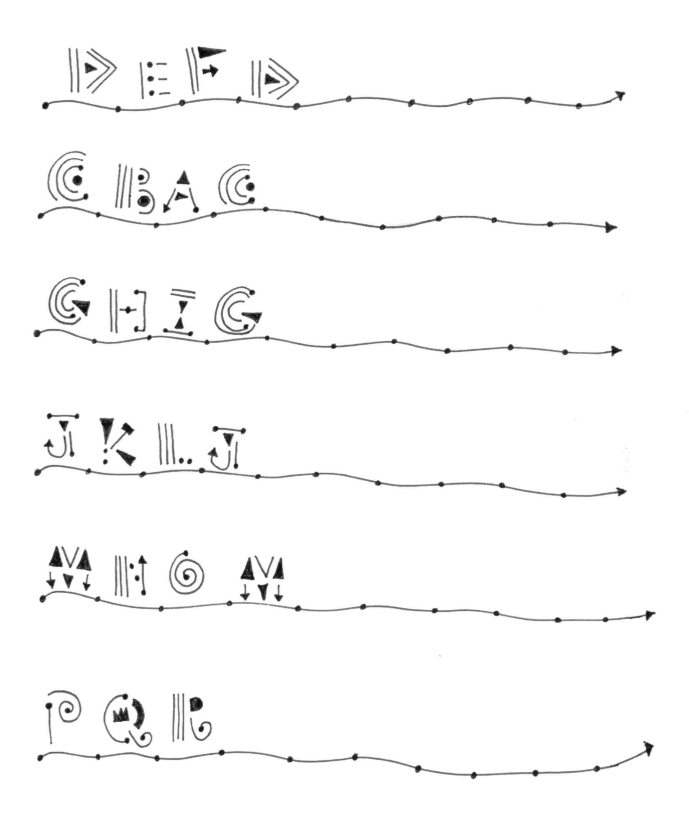

Nature Study

Go outside and make a realistic drawing of something you find in in nature.

Reading Time

Read a few pages from four books in your stack.

Copy something from each book.

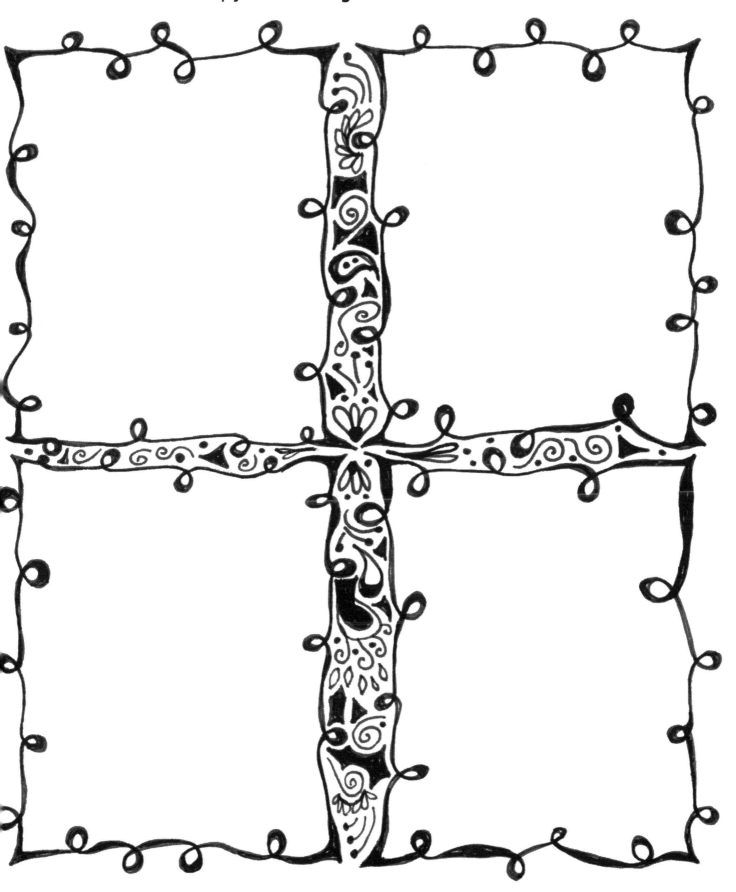

Spelling Time

Find 20 Words with 7 letters each.
Write the words here:

_____   _____

_____   _____

_____   _____

_____   _____

_____   _____

_____   _____

_____   _____

_____   _____

_____   _____

_____   _____

Start Time: _____

Stop Time: _____

Screen Time!

Watch a Documentary, Educational Program, Movie, or Tutorial.

TITLE: _____

SUBJECT _____

LOCATION: _____

YEAR: _____

MESSAGE: _____

Rating:

AWFUL

BAD

LAME

YUCKY

OKAY

NICE

GOOD

GREAT

SUPER

AMAZING

Draw a Scene from the video:

Notes:

TITLE:

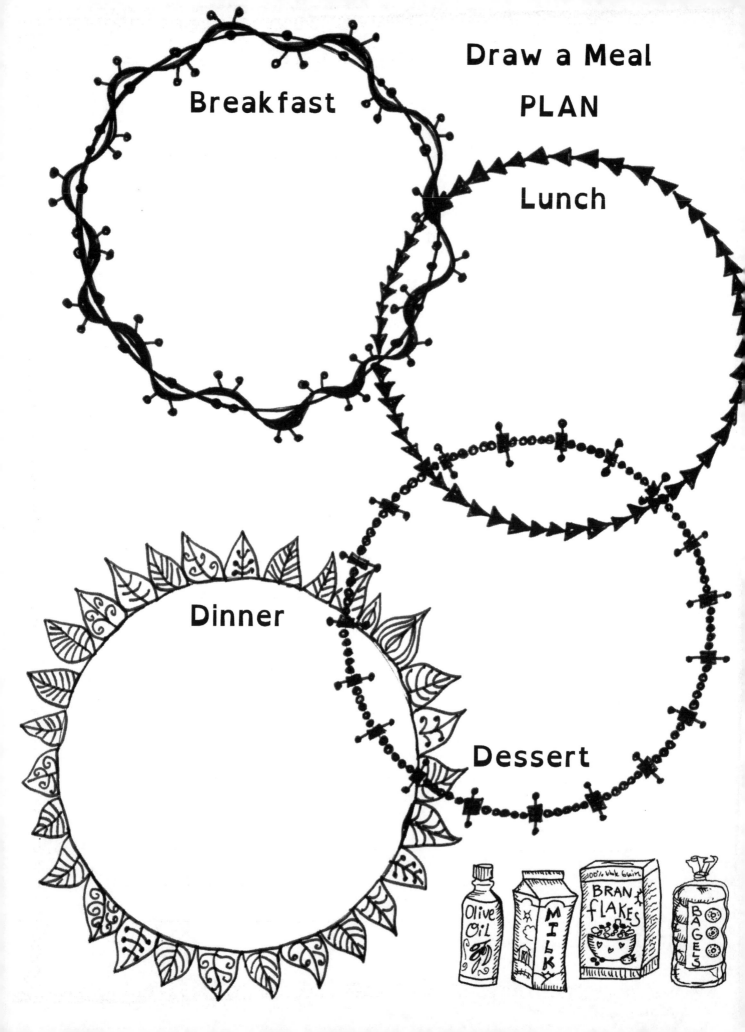

Writing Time

Stories, Poems, Lists and More.
That's what this page is waiting for!

_____

_____

_____

_____

_____

_____

_____

_____

_____

_____

_____

_____

_____

_____

_____

_____

Circle Today's Date

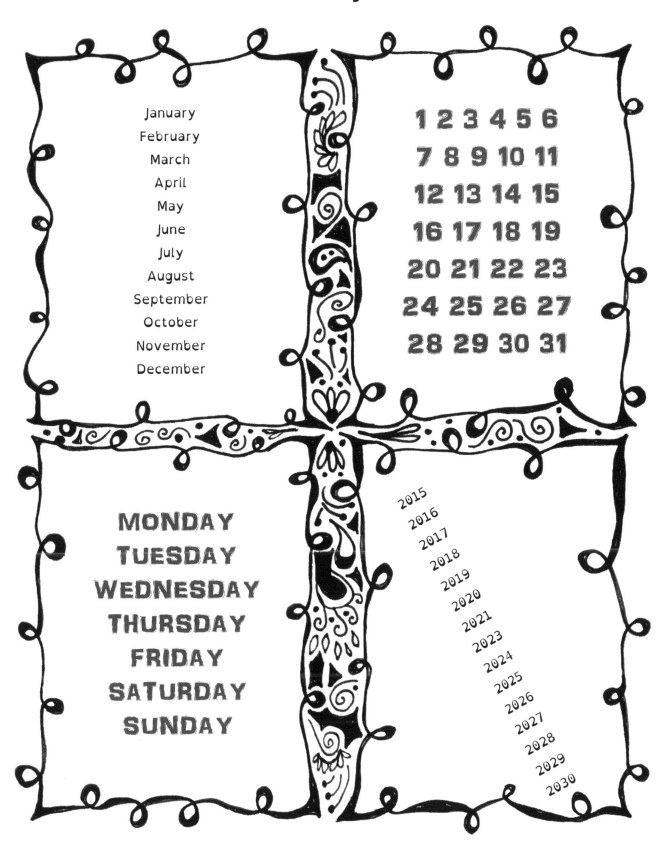

January
February
March
April
May
June
July
August
September
October
November
December

1 2 3 4 5 6
7 8 9 10 11
12 13 14 15
16 17 18 19
20 21 22 23
24 25 26 27
28 29 30 31

MONDAY
TUESDAY
WEDNESDAY
THURSDAY
FRIDAY
SATURDAY
SUNDAY

2015
2016
2017
2018
2019
2020
2021
2023
2024
2025
2026
2027
2028
2029
2030

Write Today's Date:_____

Start Your Day!

Inspirational Verse or Quote

_____
_____
_____
_____
_____

Prayer Needs

_____
_____
_____

To-Do List

_____
_____
_____
_____

Art & Logic Games

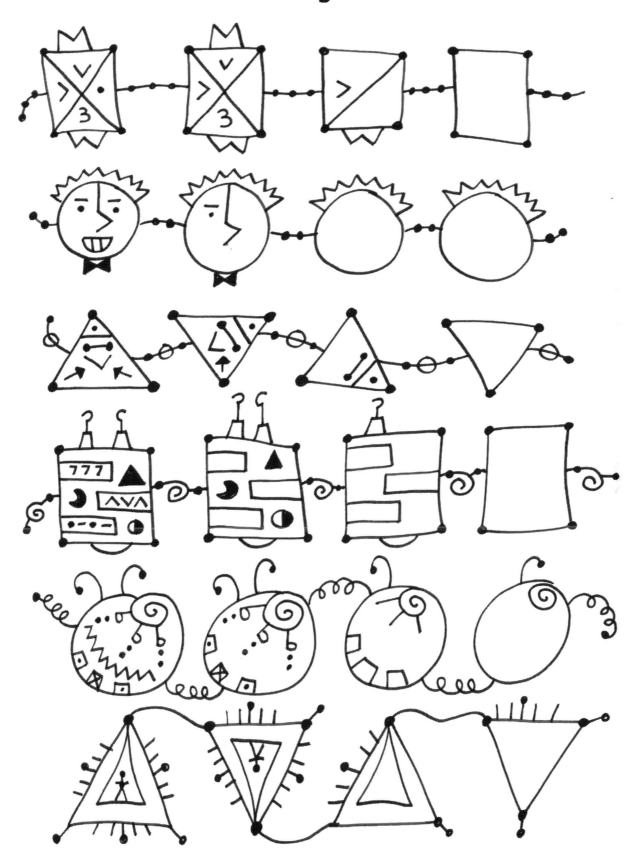

Nature Study

Go outside and make a realistic drawing of something you find in in nature.

Reading Time

Read a few pages from four books in your stack.

Copy something from each book.

Spelling Time

Find 20 Words with 6 letters each.
Write the words here:

_____   _____

_____   _____

_____   _____

_____   _____

_____   _____

_____   _____

_____   _____

_____   _____

_____   _____

_____   _____

Start Time:

_ _ _ _ _

Stop Time:

_ _ _ _ _

Screen Time!

Watch a Documentary, Educational Program, Movie, or Tutorial.

TITLE: _____

SUBJECT _____

LOCATION: _____

YEAR: _____

MESSAGE: _____

Rating:

AWFUL

BAD

LAME

YUCKY

OKAY

NICE

GOOD

GREAT

SUPER

AMAZING

Draw a Scene from the video:

Notes:

TITLE:

Writing Time

Stories, Poems, Lists and More.
That's what this page is waiting for!

_____

_____

_____

_____

_____

_____

_____

_____

_____

_____

_____

_____

_____

_____

_____

_____

_____

_____

Circle Today's Date

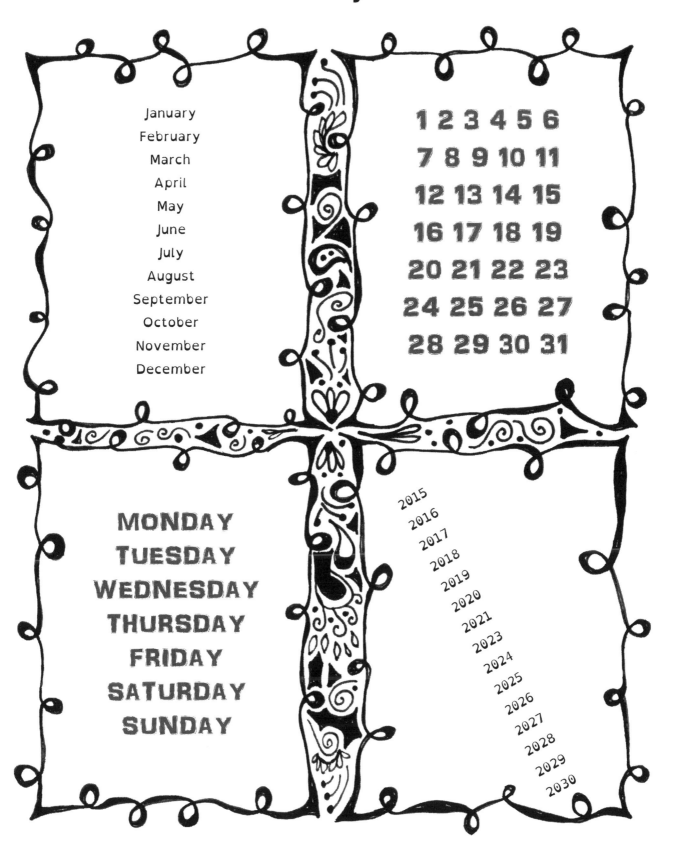

January
February
March
April
May
June
July
August
September
October
November
December

1 2 3 4 5 6
7 8 9 10 11
12 13 14 15
16 17 18 19
20 21 22 23
24 25 26 27
28 29 30 31

MONDAY
TUESDAY
WEDNESDAY
THURSDAY
FRIDAY
SATURDAY
SUNDAY

2015
2016
2017
2018
2019
2020
2021
2023
2024
2025
2026
2027
2028
2029
2030

Write Today's Date:_____

Start Your Day!

Inspirational Verse or Quote

_____

_____

_____

_____

_____

_____

Prayer Needs

_____

_____

_____

_____

To-Do List

_____

_____

_____

_____

_____

Art & Logic Games

Nature Study

Go outside and make a realistic drawing of something you find in in nature.

Reading Time

Read a few pages from four books in your stack.

Copy something from each book.

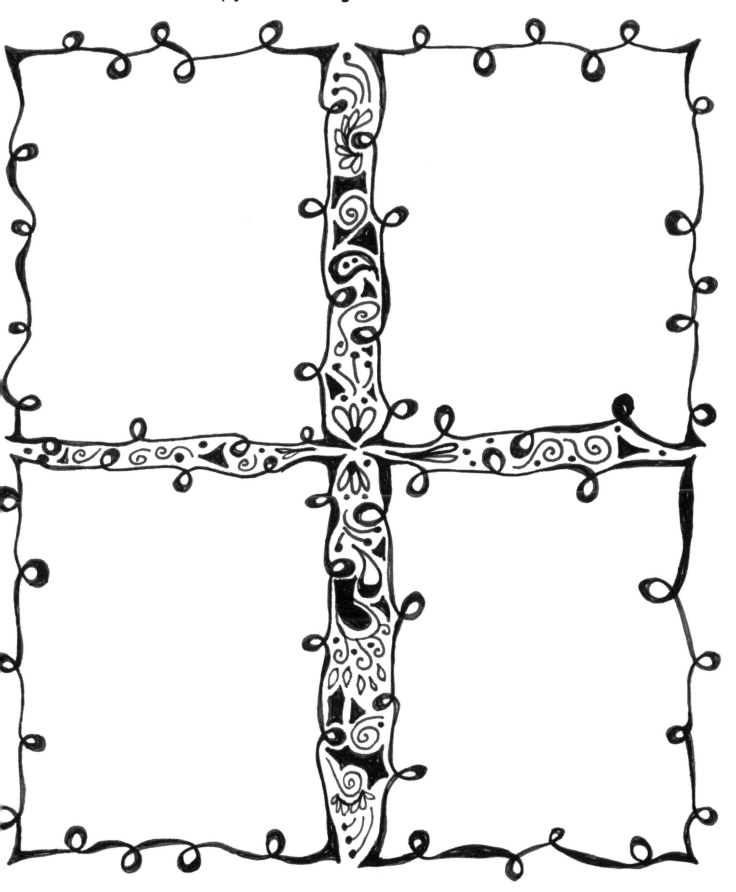

Spelling Time

Find 20 Words with 5 letters each.

Write the words here:

_____ _____

_____ _____

_____ _____

_____ _____

_____ _____

_____ _____

_____ _____

_____ _____

_____ _____

_____ _____

Start Time:

_____

Stop Time:

_____

Screen Time!

Watch a Documentary, Educational Program, Movie, or Tutorial.

TITLE: _____

SUBJECT_____

LOCATION:_____

YEAR:_____

MESSAGE: _____

Rating:

AWFUL

BAD

LAME

YUCKY

OKAY

NICE

GOOD

GREAT

SUPER

AMAZING

Notes:

TITLE:

Draw a Scene from the video:

World News Today!

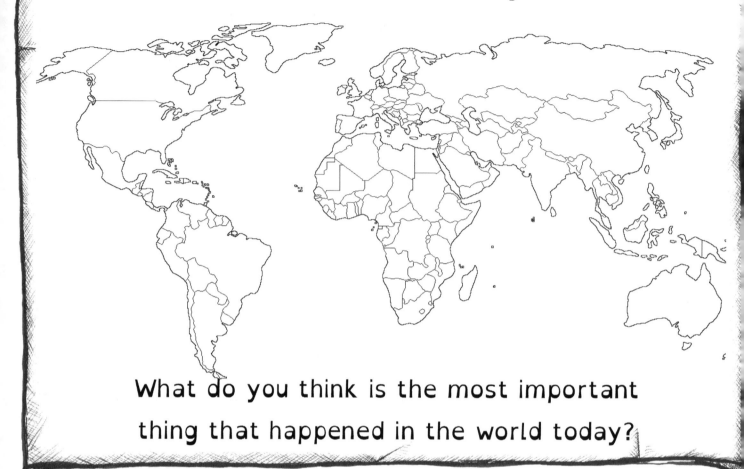

What do you think is the most important
thing that happened in the world today?

Tell the story with words or pictures.

Writing Time

Stories, Poems, Lists and More.
That's what this page is waiting for!

_____

_____

_____

_____

_____

_____

_____

_____

_____

_____

_____

_____

_____

_____

_____

_____

Circle Today's Date

January
February
March
April
May
June
July
August
September
October
November
December

1 2 3 4 5 6
7 8 9 10 11
12 13 14 15
16 17 18 19
20 21 22 23
24 25 26 27
28 29 30 31

MONDAY
TUESDAY
WEDNESDAY
THURSDAY
FRIDAY
SATURDAY
SUNDAY

2015
2016
2017
2018
2019
2020
2021
2023
2024
2025
2026
2027
2028
2029
2030

Write Today's Date:_____

Start Your Day!

Inspirational Verse or Quote

_____
_____
_____
_____
_____
_____

Prayer Needs

_____
_____
_____
_____

To-Do List

_____
_____
_____
_____
_____
_____

Art & Logic Games

Nature Study

Go outside and make a realistic drawing of something you find in in nature.

Reading Time

Read a few pages from four books in your stack.

Copy something from each book.

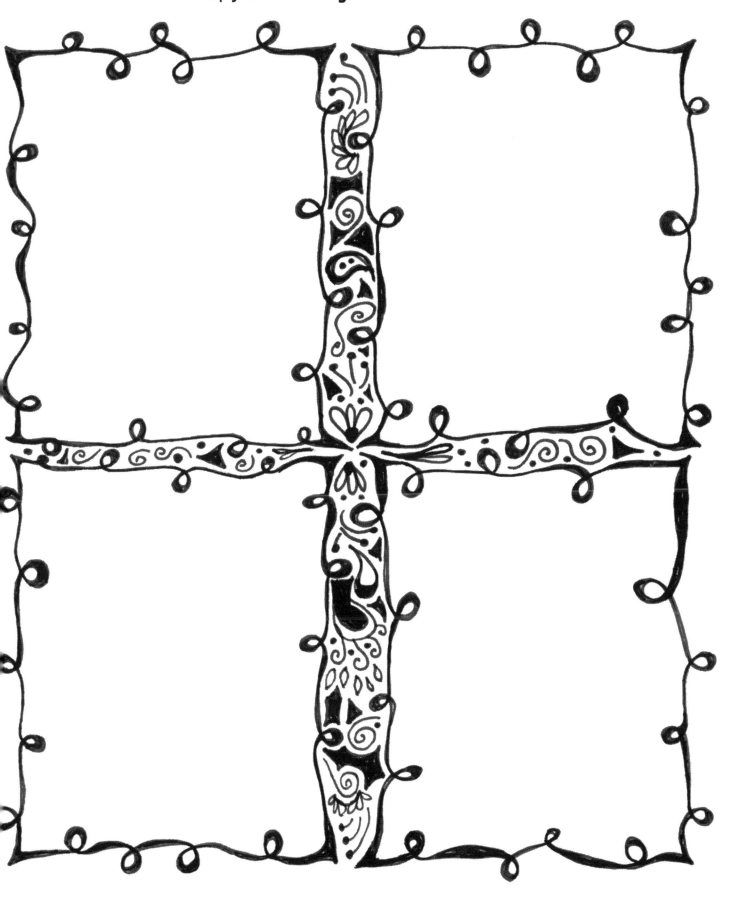

Spelling Time

Find 20 Words with 5 letters each.
Write the words here:

_____   _____

_____   _____

_____   _____

_____   _____

_____   _____

_____   _____

_____   _____

_____   _____

_____   _____

_____   _____

Screen Time!

Watch a Documentary, Educational Program, Movie, or Tutorial.

Start Time:

_ _ _ _ _

Stop Time:

_ _ _ _ _

TITLE: _____

SUBJECT _____

LOCATION: _____

YEAR: _____

MESSAGE: _____

Rating:

AWFUL

BAD

LAME

YUCKY

OKAY

NICE

GOOD

GREAT

SUPER

AMAZING

Draw a Scene from the video:

Notes:

TITLE:

DRAW THE PAST, PRESENT & FUTURE

Of _____

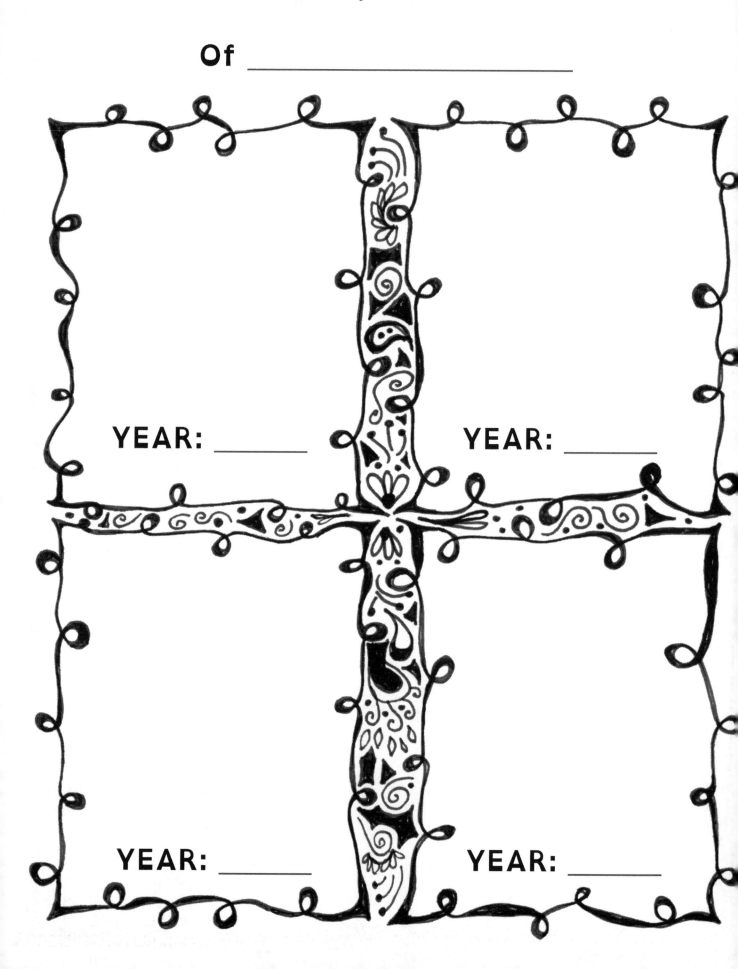

YEAR: _____

YEAR: _____

YEAR: _____

YEAR: _____

Writing Time

Stories, Poems, Lists and More.
That's what this page is waiting for!

_____

_____

_____

_____

_____

_____

_____

_____

_____

_____

_____

_____

_____

_____

_____

_____

_____

_____

Circle Today's Date

January
February
March
April
May
June
July
August
September
October
November
December

1 2 3 4 5 6
7 8 9 10 11
12 13 14 15
16 17 18 19
20 21 22 23
24 25 26 27
28 29 30 31

MONDAY
TUESDAY
WEDNESDAY
THURSDAY
FRIDAY
SATURDAY
SUNDAY

2015
2016
2017
2018
2019
2020
2021
2023
2024
2025
2026
2027
2028
2029
2030

Write Today's Date:_____

Start Your Day!

Inspirational Verse or Quote

_____
_____
_____
_____
_____
_____

Prayer Needs

_____
_____
_____
_____

To-Do List

_____
_____
_____
_____
_____

Art & Logic Games

Nature Study

Go outside and make a realistic drawing of something you find in in nature.

Reading Time

Read a few pages from four books in your stack.

Copy something from each book.

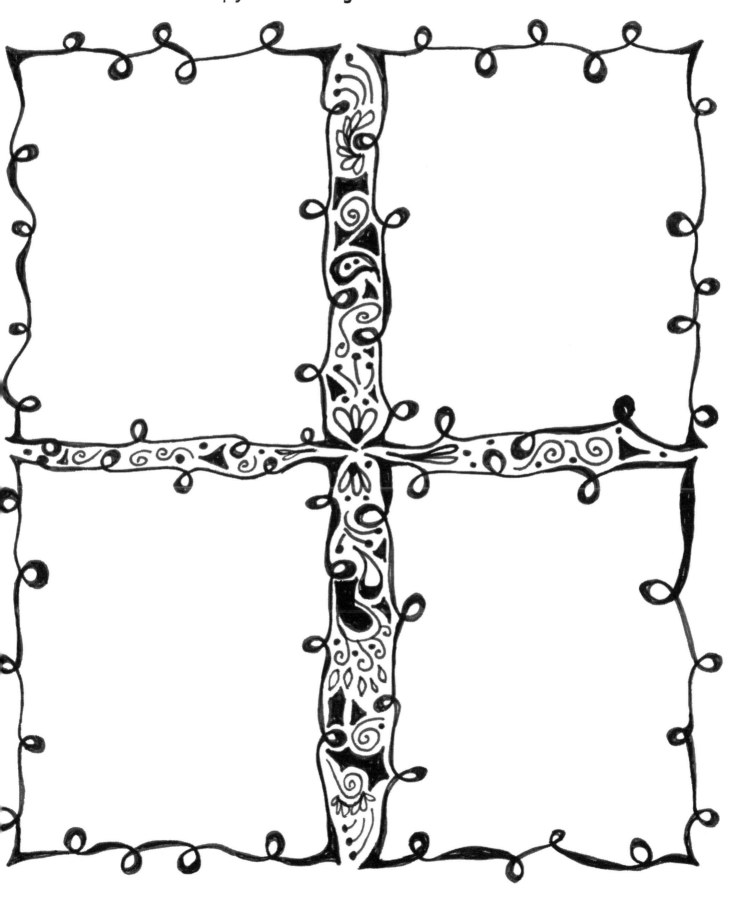

Spelling Time

Find 20 Words with 4 letters each.
Write the words here:

_____   _____

_____   _____

_____   _____

_____   _____

_____   _____

_____   _____

_____   _____

_____   _____

_____   _____

_____   _____

Screen Time!

Start Time:

_ _ _ _ _

Stop Time:

_ _ _ _ _

Watch a Documentary, Educational Program, Movie, or Tutorial.

TITLE: _____

SUBJECT _____

LOCATION: _____

YEAR: _____

MESSAGE: _____

Rating:

AWFUL

BAD

LAME

YUCKY

OKAY

NICE

GOOD

GREAT

SUPER

AMAZING

Draw a Scene from the video:

Notes:

TITLE:

Listening Time

Listen to an audio book or classical music or ask someone to read a story to you while you color and draw on the next page.

What are you listening to?

_____

Circle Today's Date

January
February
March
April
May
June
July
August
September
October
November
December

1 2 3 4 5 6
7 8 9 10 11
12 13 14 15
16 17 18 19
20 21 22 23
24 25 26 27
28 29 30 31

MONDAY
TUESDAY
WEDNESDAY
THURSDAY
FRIDAY
SATURDAY
SUNDAY

2015
2016
2017
2018
2019
2020
2021
2023
2024
2025
2026
2027
2028
2029
2030

Write Today's Date:_____

Start Your Day!

Inspirational Verse or Quote

_____

_____

_____

_____

_____

_____

Prayer Needs

_____

_____

_____

_____

To-Do List

_____

_____

_____

_____

_____

Art & Logic Games

Nature Study

Go outside and make a realistic drawing of something you find in in nature.

Reading Time

Read a few pages from four books in your stack.

Copy something from each book.

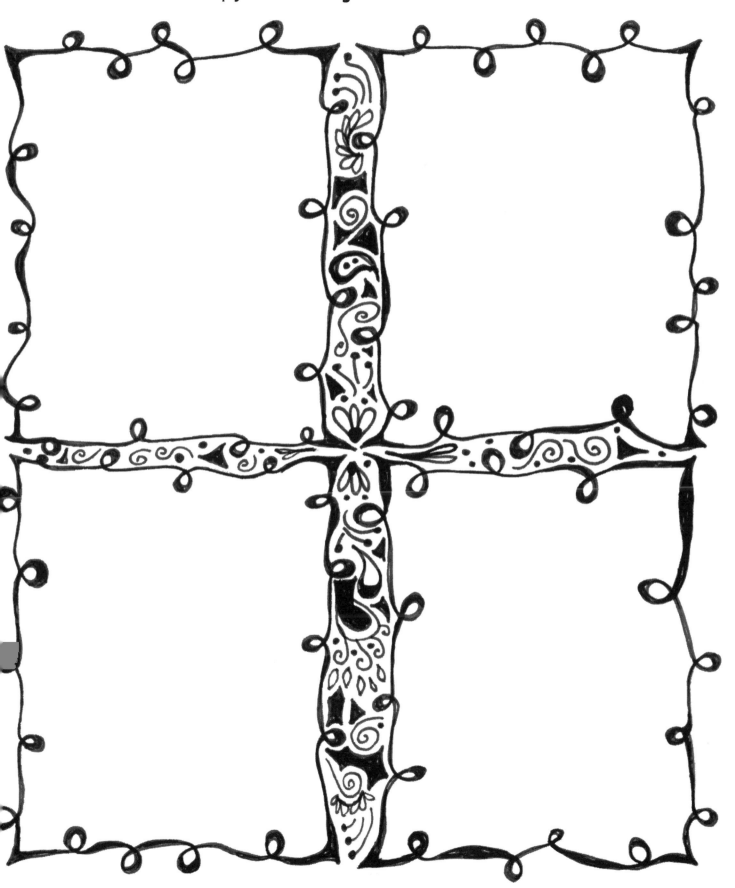

Spelling Time

Find 20 Words with 3 letters each.
Write the words here:

_____   _____

_____   _____

_____   _____

_____   _____

_____   _____

_____   _____

_____   _____

_____   _____

_____   _____

_____   _____

Screen Time!

Watch a Documentary, Educational Program, Movie, or Tutorial.

Start Time: _____

Stop Time: _____

TITLE: _____

SUBJECT _____

LOCATION: _____

YEAR: _____

MESSAGE: _____

Rating:

AWFUL

BAD

LAME

YUCKY

OKAY

NICE

GOOD

GREAT

SUPER

AMAZING

Draw a Scene from the video:

Notes:

TITLE:

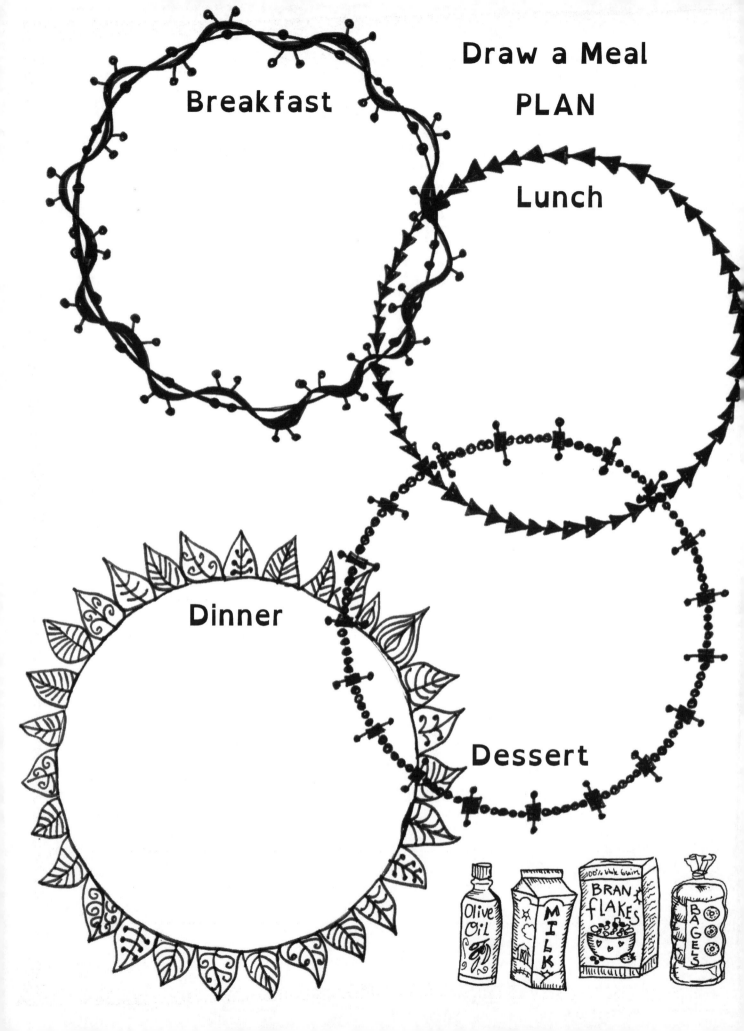

Breakfast

Draw a Meal
PLAN

Lunch

Dinner

Dessert

Writing Time

Stories, Poems, Lists and More.
That's what this page is waiting for!

_____

_____

_____

_____

_____

_____

_____

_____

_____

_____

_____

_____

_____

_____

_____

Circle Today's Date

January
February
March
April
May
June
July
August
September
October
November
December

1 2 3 4 5 6
7 8 9 10 11
12 13 14 15
16 17 18 19
20 21 22 23
24 25 26 27
28 29 30 31

MONDAY
TUESDAY
WEDNESDAY
THURSDAY
FRIDAY
SATURDAY
SUNDAY

2015
2016
2017
2018
2019
2020
2021
2023
2024
2025
2026
2027
2028
2029
2030

Write Today's Date:_____

Start Your Day!

Inspirational Verse or Quote

_____

_____

_____

_____

_____

_____

Prayer Needs

_____

_____

_____

To-Do List

_____

_____

_____

_____

_____

Art & Logic Games

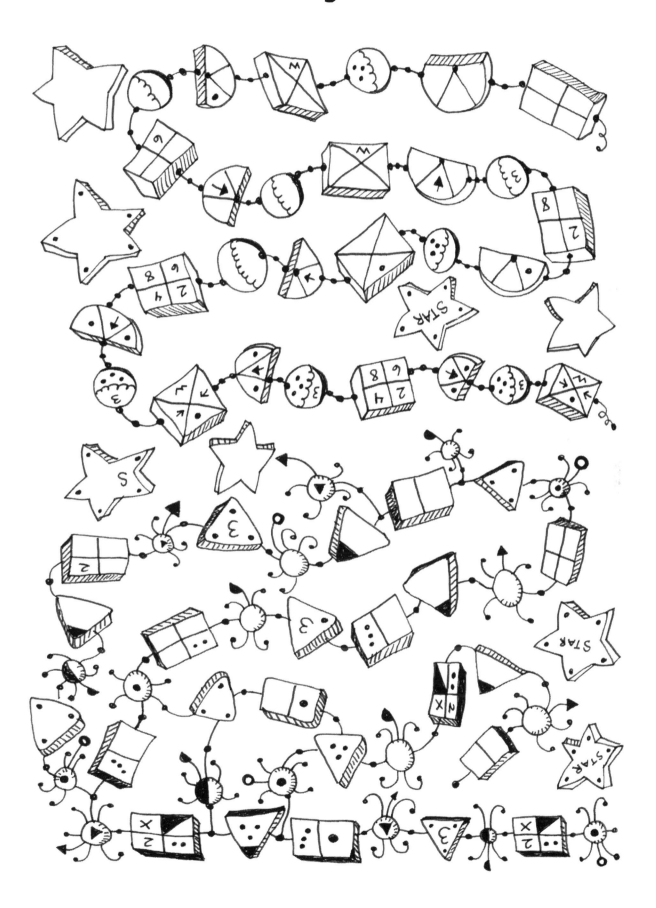

Nature Study

Go outside and make a realistic
drawing of something you find in
in nature.

Reading Time

Read a few pages from four books in your stack.

Copy something from each book.

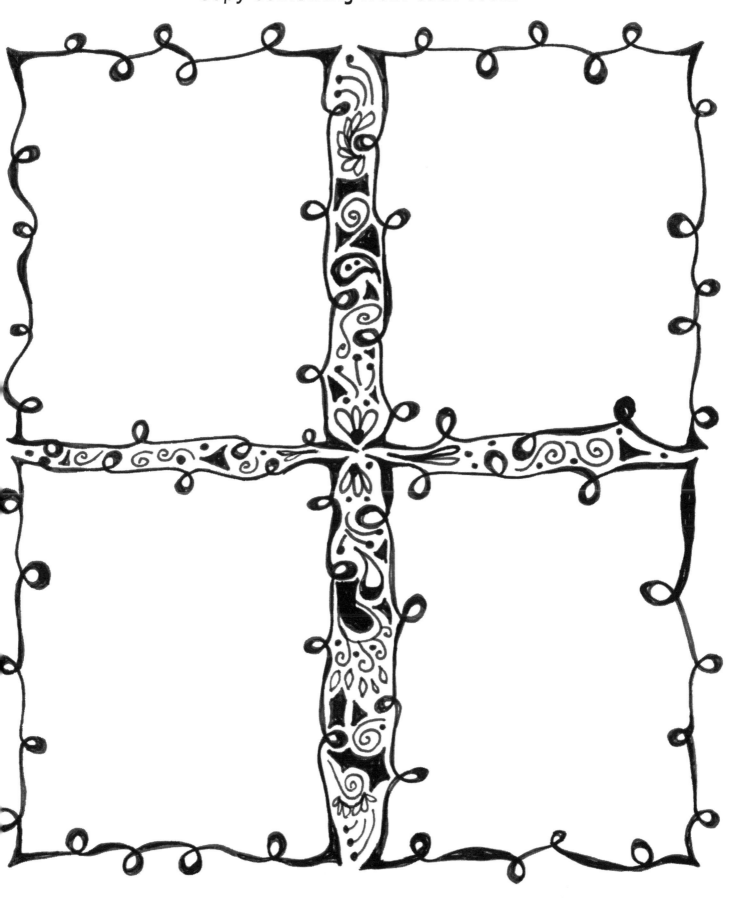

Spelling Time

Find 20 Words with 4 letters each.

Write the words here:

_____   _____

_____   _____

_____   _____

_____   _____

_____   _____

_____   _____

_____   _____

_____   _____

_____   _____

_____   _____

Screen Time!

Watch a Documentary, Educational Program, Movie, or Tutorial.

Start Time:

_ _ _ _ _

Stop Time:

_ _ _ _ _

TITLE: _____

SUBJECT_____

LOCATION:_____

YEAR:_____

MESSAGE: _____

Rating:

AWFUL

BAD

LAME

YUCKY

OKAY

NICE

GOOD

GREAT

SUPER

AMAZING

Draw a Scene from the video:

Notes:

TITLE:

Writing Time

Stories, Poems, Lists and More.
That's what this page is waiting for!

_____

_____

_____

_____

_____

_____

_____

_____

_____

_____

_____

_____

_____

_____

_____

_____

_____

Circle Today's Date

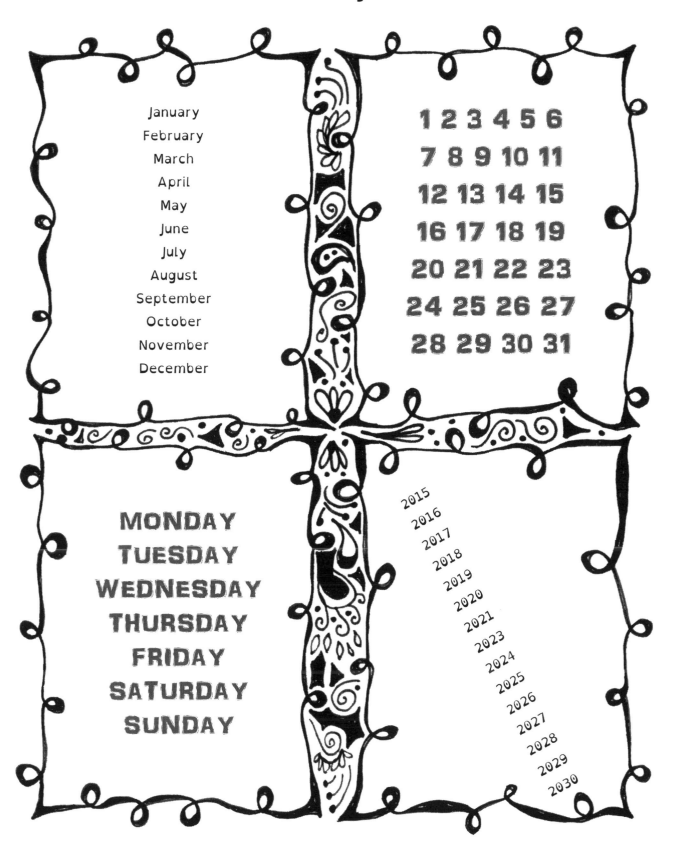

January
February
March
April
May
June
July
August
September
October
November
December

1 2 3 4 5 6
7 8 9 10 11
12 13 14 15
16 17 18 19
20 21 22 23
24 25 26 27
28 29 30 31

MONDAY
TUESDAY
WEDNESDAY
THURSDAY
FRIDAY
SATURDAY
SUNDAY

2015
2016
2017
2018
2019
2020
2021
2023
2024
2025
2026
2027
2028
2029
2030

Write Today's Date:_____

Start Your Day!

Inspirational Verse or Quote

_____

_____

_____

_____

_____

_____

Prayer Needs

_____

_____

_____

_____

To-Do List

_____

_____

_____

_____

_____

Art & Logic Games

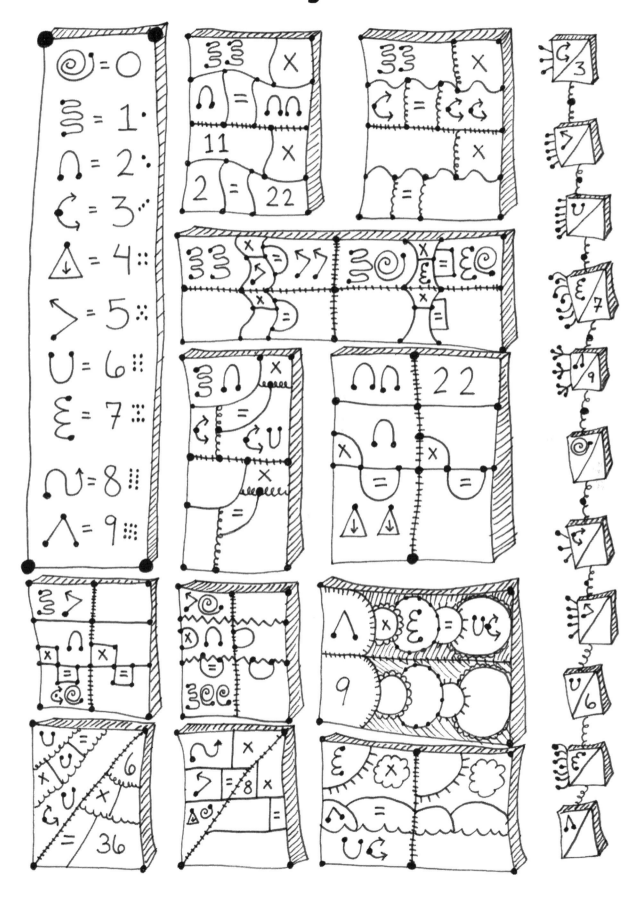

Nature Study

Go outside and make a realistic drawing of something you find in in nature.

Reading Time

Read a few pages from four books in your stack.

Copy something from each book.

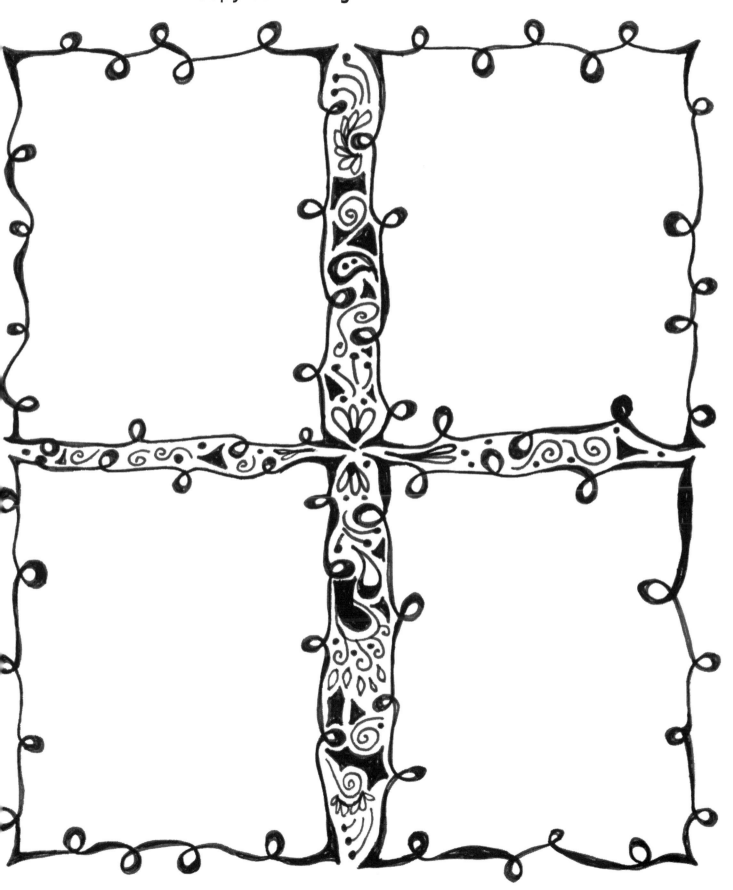

Spelling Time

Find 20 Words with 5 letters each.
Write the words here:

_____   _____

_____   _____

_____   _____

_____   _____

_____   _____

_____   _____

_____   _____

_____   _____

_____   _____

_____   _____

Writing Time

Stories, Poems, Lists and More.
That's what this page is waiting for!

_____

_____

_____

_____

_____

_____

_____

_____

_____

_____

_____

_____

_____

_____

_____

_____

_____

_____

_____

_____

Circle Today's Date

January
February
March
April
May
June
July
August
September
October
November
December

1 2 3 4 5 6
7 8 9 10 11
12 13 14 15
16 17 18 19
20 21 22 23
24 25 26 27
28 29 30 31

MONDAY
TUESDAY
WEDNESDAY
THURSDAY
FRIDAY
SATURDAY
SUNDAY

2015
2016
2017
2018
2019
2020
2021
2023
2024
2025
2026
2027
2028
2029
2030

Write Today's Date:_____

Start Your Day!

Inspirational Verse or Quote

_____

_____

_____

_____

_____

_____

Prayer Needs

_____

_____

_____

To-Do List

_____

_____

_____

_____

_____

Art & Logic Games

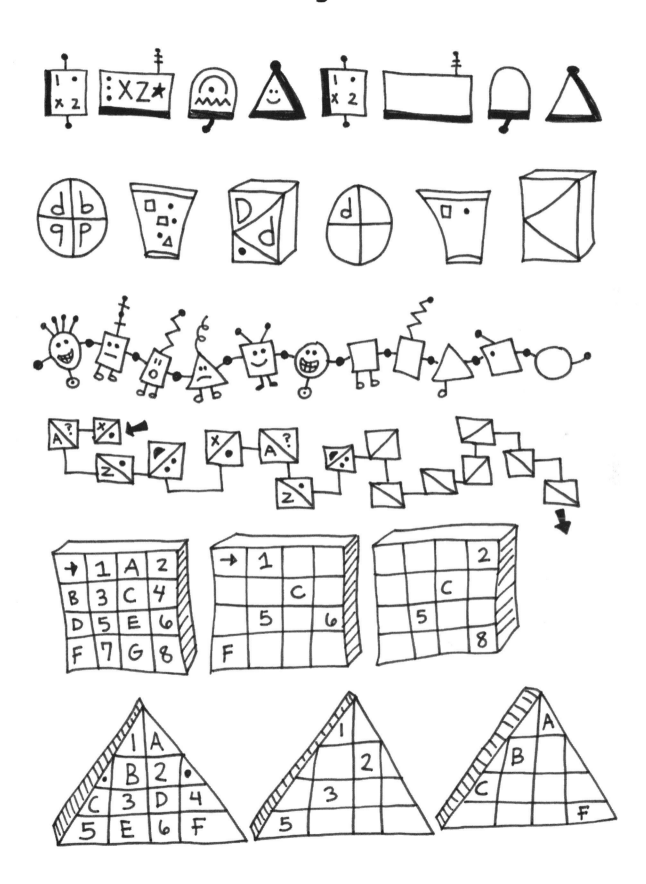

Nature Study

Go outside and make a realistic
drawing of something you find in
in nature.

Reading Time

Read a few pages from four books in your stack.

Copy something from each book.

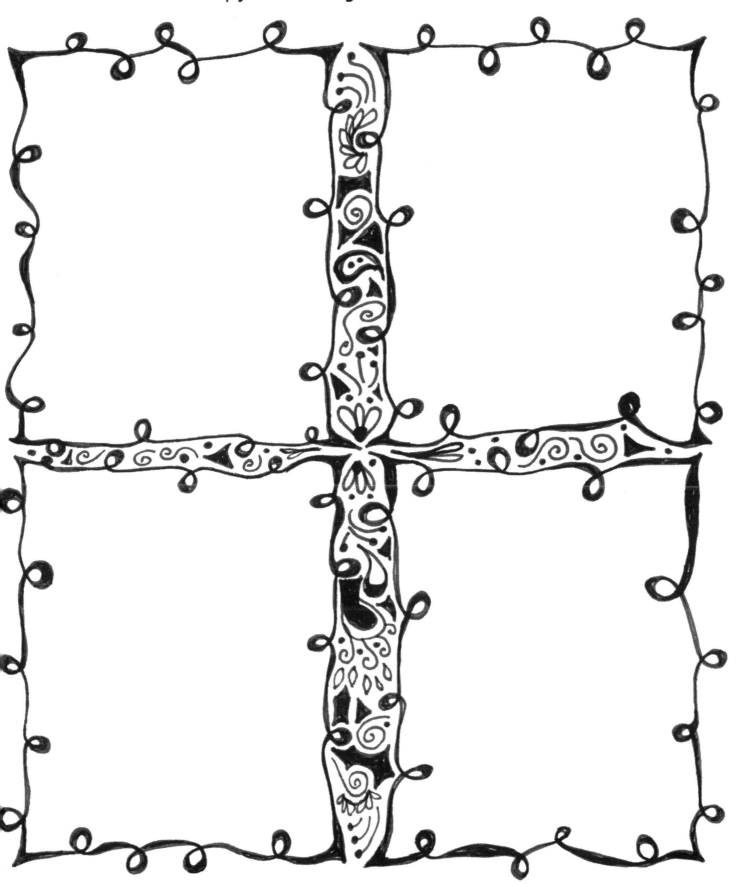

Spelling Time

Find 20 Words with 6 letters each.

Write the words here:

_____   _____

_____   _____

_____   _____

_____   _____

_____   _____

_____   _____

_____   _____

_____   _____

_____   _____

_____   _____

Start Time: _ _ _ _ _

Stop Time: _ _ _ _ _

Screen Time!

Watch a Documentary, Educational Program, Movie, or Tutorial.

TITLE: _____

SUBJECT _____

LOCATION: _____

YEAR: _____

MESSAGE: _____

Rating:

AWFUL

BAD

LAME

YUCKY

OKAY

NICE

GOOD

GREAT

SUPER

AMAZING

Draw a Scene from the video:

Notes:

TITLE:

World News Today!

What do you think is the most important
thing that happened in the world today?

Tell the story with words or pictures.

Writing Time

Stories, Poems, Lists and More.

That's what this page is waiting for!

_____

_____

_____

_____

_____

_____

_____

_____

_____

_____

_____

_____

_____

_____

_____

_____

_____

_____

Circle Today's Date

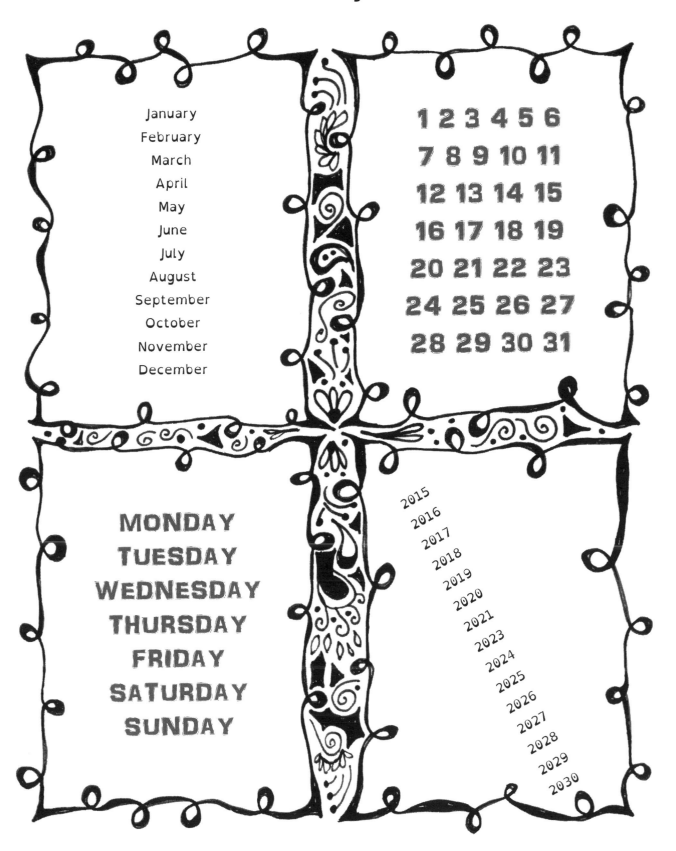

January
February
March
April
May
June
July
August
September
October
November
December

1 2 3 4 5 6
7 8 9 10 11
12 13 14 15
16 17 18 19
20 21 22 23
24 25 26 27
28 29 30 31

MONDAY
TUESDAY
WEDNESDAY
THURSDAY
FRIDAY
SATURDAY
SUNDAY

2015
2016
2017
2018
2019
2020
2021
2023
2024
2025
2026
2027
2028
2029
2030

Write Today's Date:_____

Start Your Day!

Inspirational Verse or Quote

_____

_____

_____

_____

_____

_____

Prayer Needs

_____

_____

_____

To-Do List

_____

_____

_____

_____

_____

Art & Logic Games

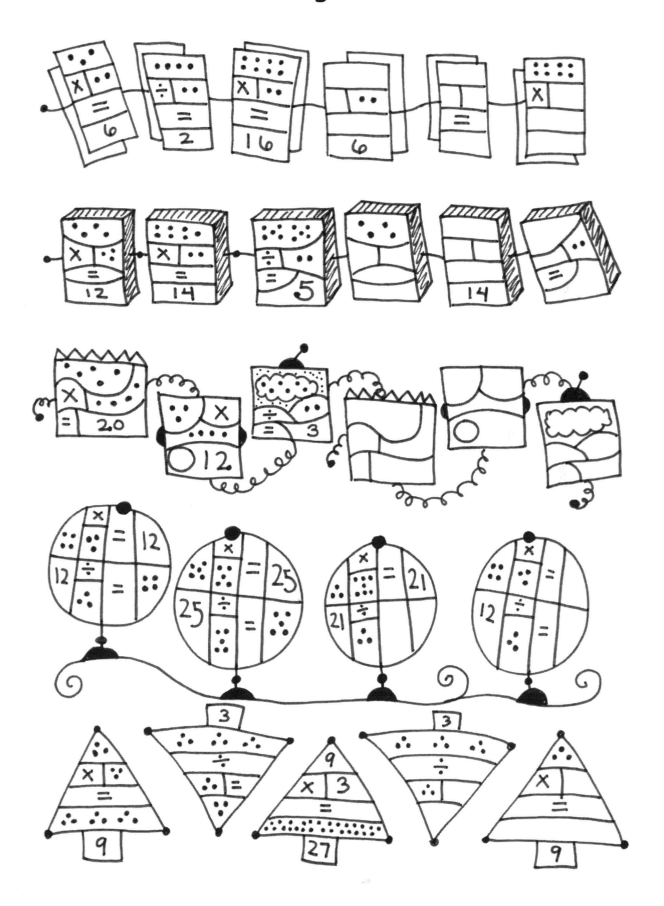

Nature Study

Go outside and make a realistic drawing of something you find in in nature.

Reading Time

Read a few pages from four books in your stack.

Copy something from each book.

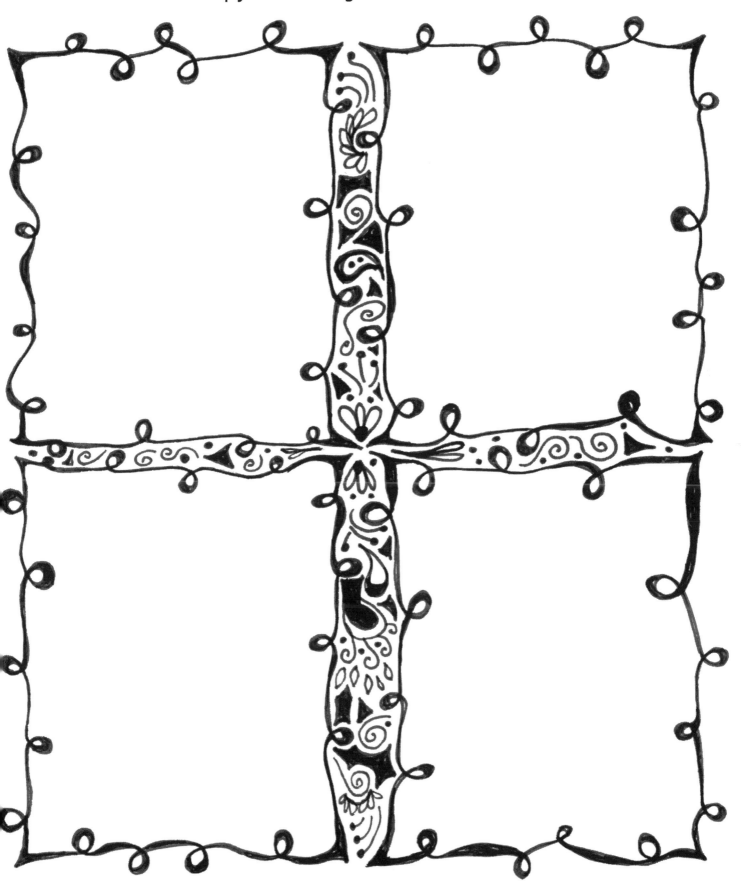

Spelling Time

Find 20 Words with *7* letters each.

Write the words here:

Writing Time

Stories, Poems, Lists and More.

That's what this page is waiting for!

_____

_____

_____

_____

_____

_____

_____

_____

_____

_____

_____

_____

_____

_____

_____

_____

_____

_____

_____

Circle Today's Date

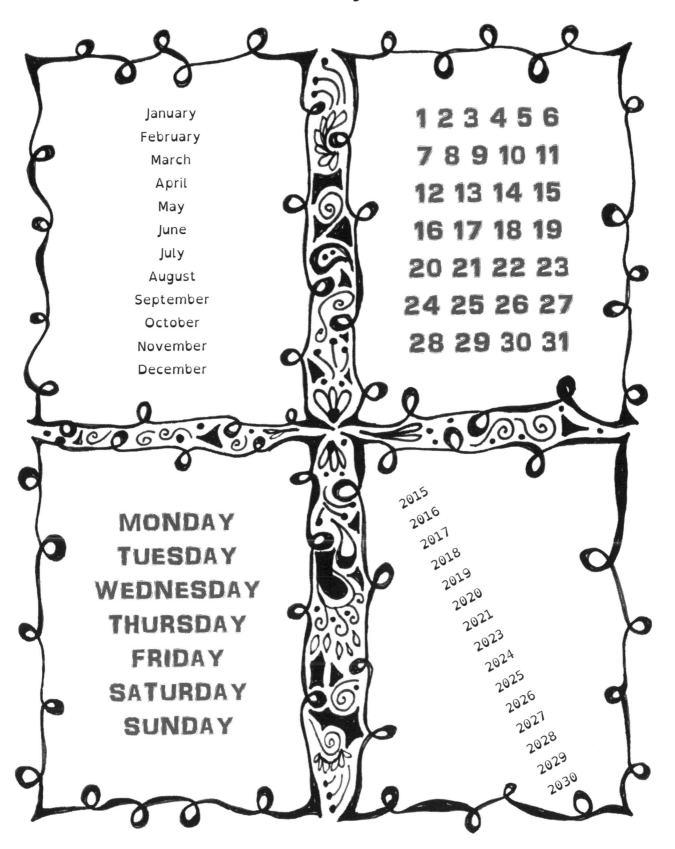

January
February
March
April
May
June
July
August
September
October
November
December

1 2 3 4 5 6
7 8 9 10 11
12 13 14 15
16 17 18 19
20 21 22 23
24 25 26 27
28 29 30 31

MONDAY
TUESDAY
WEDNESDAY
THURSDAY
FRIDAY
SATURDAY
SUNDAY

2015
2016
2017
2018
2019
2020
2021
2023
2024
2025
2026
2027
2028
2029
2030

Write Today's Date:_____

Start Your Day!

Inspirational Verse or Quote

_____

_____

_____

_____

_____

_____

Prayer Needs

_____

_____

_____

To-Do List

_____

_____

_____

_____

_____

Art & Logic Games

Nature Study

Go outside and make a realistic drawing of something you find in in nature.

Reading Time

Read a few pages from four books in your stack.

Copy something from each book.

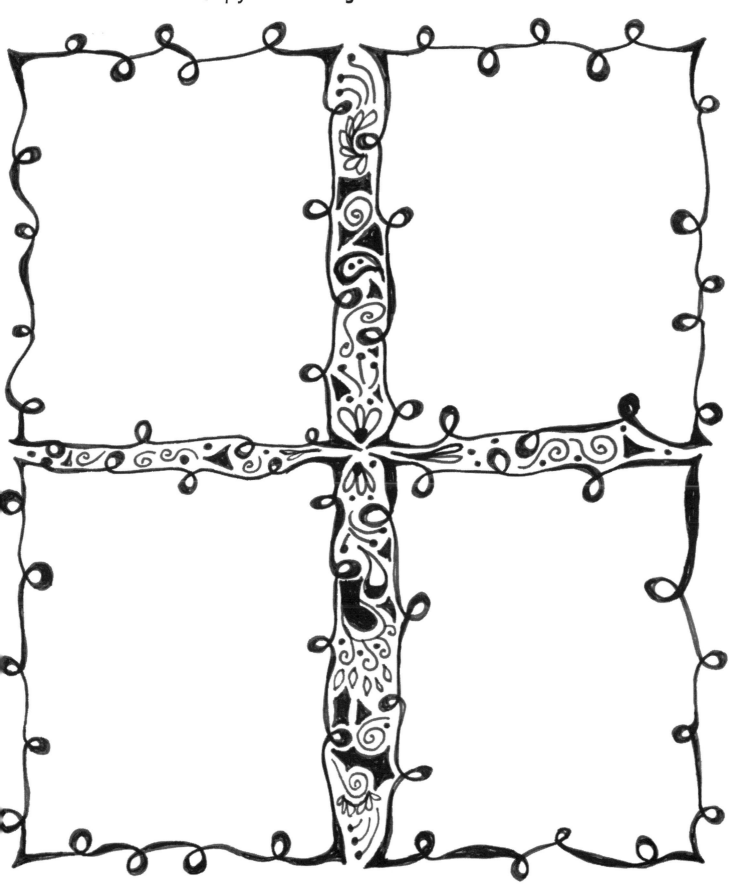

Spelling Time

Find 20 Words with 8 letters each.

Write the words here:

Start Time:

Stop Time:

Screen Time!

Watch a Documentary, Educational Program, Movie, or Tutorial.

TITLE: _____

SUBJECT _____

LOCATION: _____

YEAR: _____

MESSAGE: _____

Rating:

AWFUL

BAD

LAME

YUCKY

OKAY

NICE

GOOD

GREAT

SUPER

AMAZING

Notes:

Draw a Scene from the video:

TITLE:

Listening Time

Listen to an audio book or classical music or ask someone to read a story to you while you color and draw on the next page.

What are you listening to?

_____

Circle Today's Date

January
February
March
April
May
June
July
August
September
October
November
December

1 2 3 4 5 6
7 8 9 10 11
12 13 14 15
16 17 18 19
20 21 22 23
24 25 26 27
28 29 30 31

MONDAY
TUESDAY
WEDNESDAY
THURSDAY
FRIDAY
SATURDAY
SUNDAY

2015
2016
2017
2018
2019
2020
2021
2023
2024
2025
2026
2027
2028
2029
2030

Write Today's Date:_____

Start Your Day!

Inspirational Verse or Quote

_____

_____

_____

_____

_____

_____

Prayer Needs

_____

_____

_____

To-Do List

_____

_____

_____

_____

_____

Art & Logic Games

Nature Study

Go outside and make a realistic
drawing of something you find in
in nature.

Reading Time

Read a few pages from four books in your stack.
Copy something from each book.

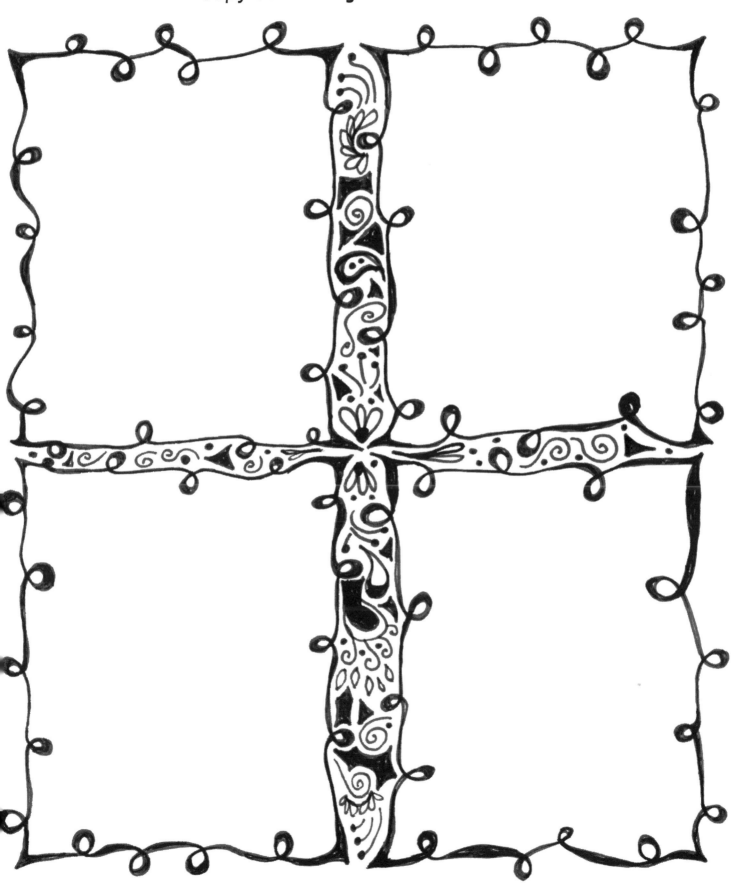

Spelling Time

Find 20 Words with 9 letters each.

Write the words here:

_____   _____

_____   _____

_____   _____

_____   _____

_____   _____

_____   _____

_____   _____

_____   _____

_____   _____

_____   _____

Screen Time!

Watch a Documentary, Educational Program, Movie, or Tutorial.

Start Time:
_ _ _ _ _

Stop Time:
_ _ _ _ _

TITLE: _____

SUBJECT _____

LOCATION: _____

YEAR: _____

MESSAGE: _____

Rating:

AWFUL

BAD

LAME

YUCKY

OKAY

NICE

GOOD

GREAT

SUPER

AMAZING

Draw a Scene from the video:

Notes:

TITLE:

World News Today!

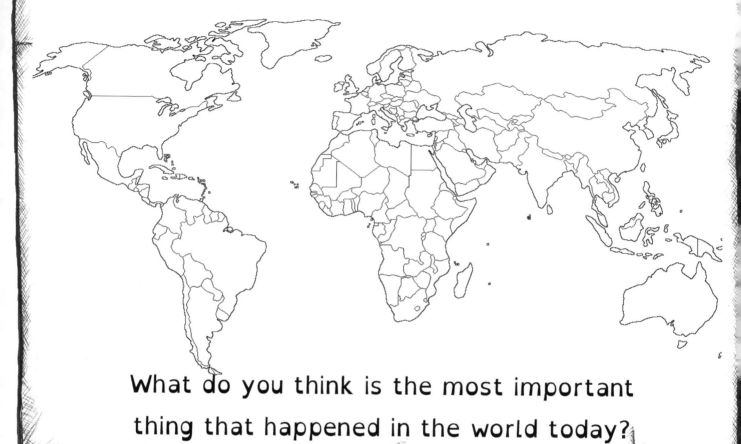

What do you think is the most important thing that happened in the world today?

Tell the story with words or pictures.

Writing Time

Stories, Poems, Lists and More.

That's what this page is waiting for!

_____

_____

_____

_____

_____

_____

_____

_____

_____

_____

_____

_____

_____

_____

_____

_____

_____

_____

Circle Today's Date

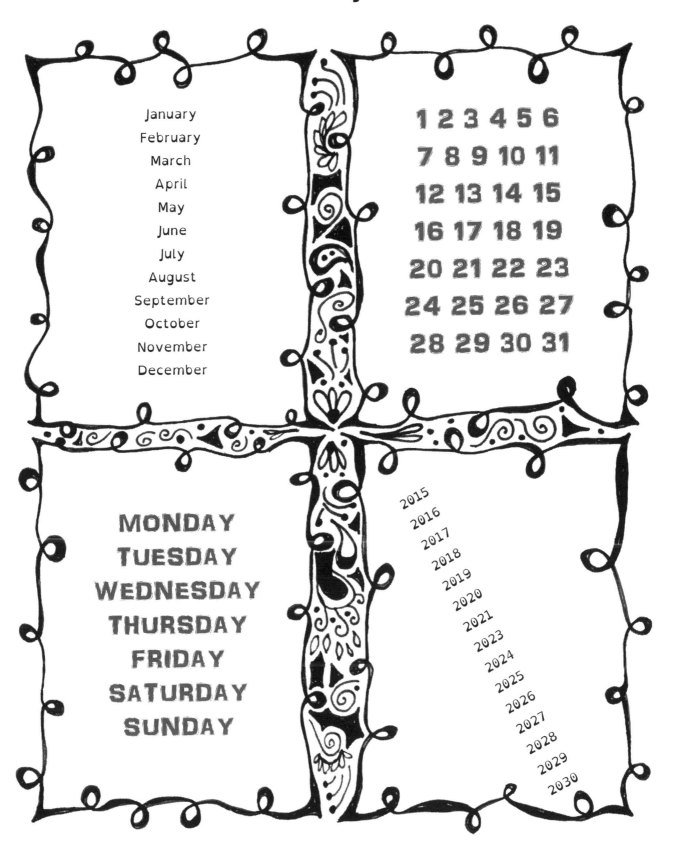

January
February
March
April
May
June
July
August
September
October
November
December

1 2 3 4 5 6
7 8 9 10 11
12 13 14 15
16 17 18 19
20 21 22 23
24 25 26 27
28 29 30 31

MONDAY
TUESDAY
WEDNESDAY
THURSDAY
FRIDAY
SATURDAY
SUNDAY

2015
2016
2017
2018
2019
2020
2021
2023
2024
2025
2026
2027
2028
2029
2030

Write Today's Date:_____

Start Your Day!

Inspirational Verse or Quote

_____

_____

_____

_____

_____

_____

Prayer Needs

_____

_____

_____

To-Do List

_____

_____

_____

_____

Art & Logic Games

Symbol	Value
😊	⃝
🚶	= 1
🌸	= 2
🌙	= 3
⭐	= 4
☀	= 5
🌳	= 6
☕	= 7
🧁	= 8
🧊	= 9

Row 1

🌙	
⭐ x	x
12	

🌙	
☀ x	
15	

🌙	
🌳 x	x
18	

🌙	
🧁 x	
24	

🌙	
☕ x	x
21	

Row 2

⭐	
⭐ x	x
16	

⭐	
🌳 x	x
24	

⭐	
🧁 x	x
32	

⭐	
☕ x	x
28	

⭐	
🧊 x	x
36	

Row 3

☀	
☀ x	x
25	

☀	
🌳 x	x
30	

☀	
🧊 x	x
45	

☀	
☕ x	x
35	

☀	
🧁 x	x
40	

Row 4

🌳	
🌳 x	x
36	

🌳	
☕ x	x
42	

🌳	
🧊 x	x
54	

🌳	
🧁 x	x
48	

🌳	
⭐ x	x
24	

Nature Study

Go outside and make a realistic drawing of something you find in in nature.

Reading Time

Read a few pages from four books in your stack.
Copy something from each book.

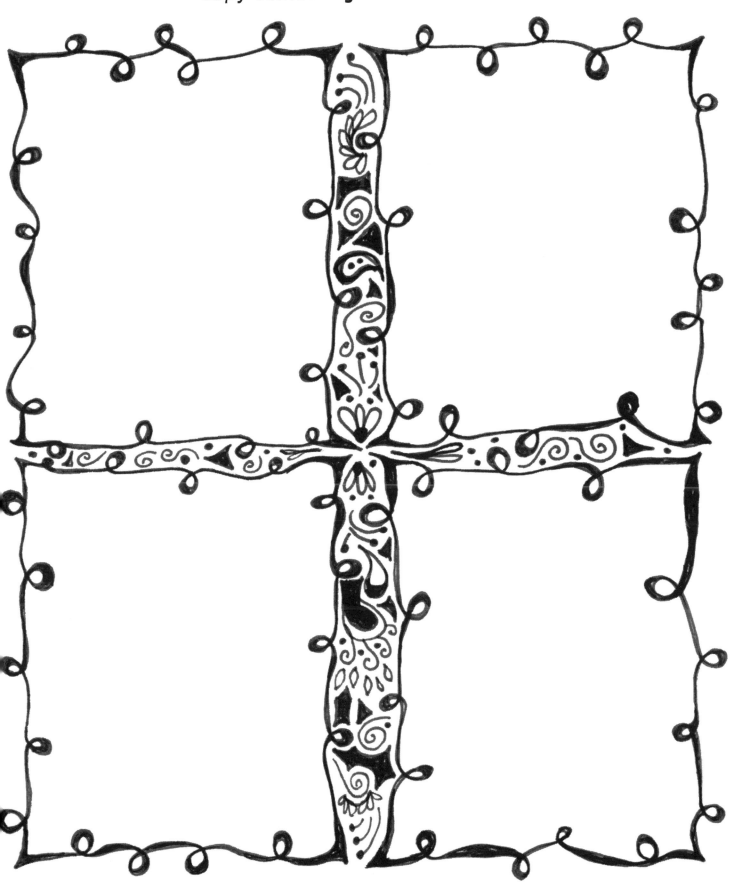

Spelling Time

Find 20 Words with **8** letters each.

Write the words here:

_____   _____

_____   _____

_____   _____

_____   _____

_____   _____

_____   _____

_____   _____

_____   _____

_____   _____

_____   _____

Screen Time!

Watch a Documentary, Educational Program, Movie, or Tutorial.

Start Time:
_ _ _ _ _

Stop Time:
_ _ _ _ _

TITLE: _____
SUBJECT _____
LOCATION: _____
YEAR: _____
MESSAGE: _____

Rating:
AWFUL
BAD
LAME
YUCKY
OKAY
NICE
GOOD
GREAT
SUPER
AMAZING

Draw a Scene from the video:

Notes:

TITLE:

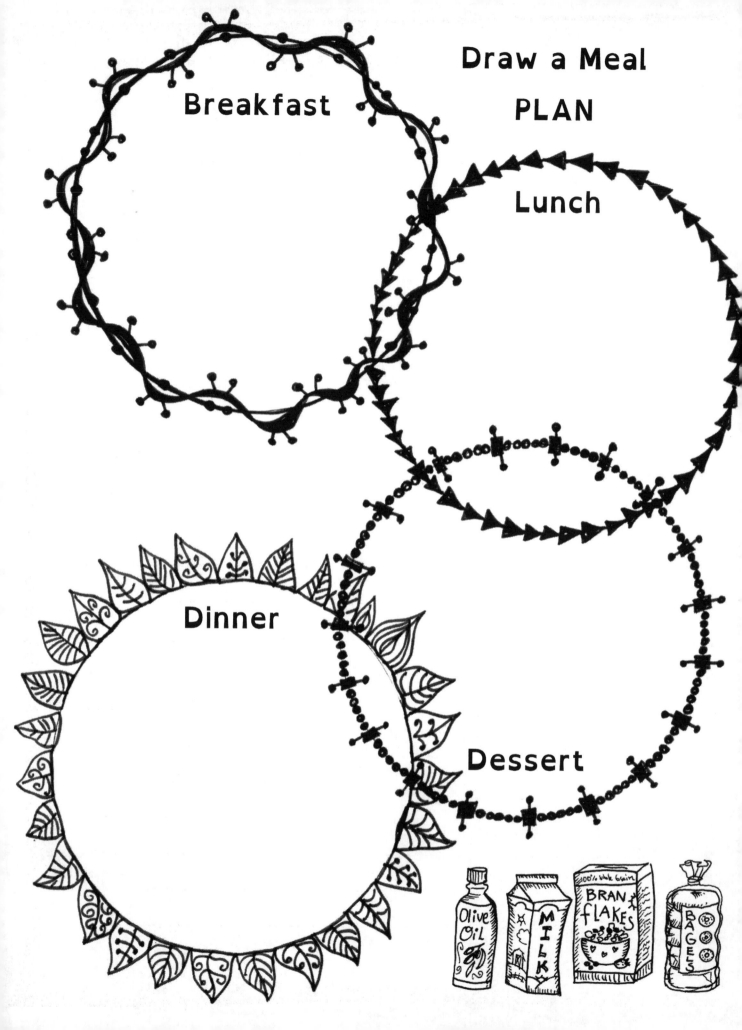

Breakfast

Draw a Meal
PLAN

Lunch

Dinner

Dessert

Writing Time

Stories, Poems, Lists and More.

That's what this page is waiting for!

Circle Today's Date

January
February
March
April
May
June
July
August
September
October
November
December

1 2 3 4 5 6
7 8 9 10 11
12 13 14 15
16 17 18 19
20 21 22 23
24 25 26 27
28 29 30 31

MONDAY
TUESDAY
WEDNESDAY
THURSDAY
FRIDAY
SATURDAY
SUNDAY

2015
2016
2017
2018
2019
2020
2021
2023
2024
2025
2026
2027
2028
2029
2030

Write Today's Date:_____

Start Your Day!

Inspirational Verse or Quote

_____

_____

_____

_____

_____

_____

Prayer Needs

_____

_____

_____

To-Do List

_____

_____

_____

_____

_____

_____

Art & Logic Games

Two
T__ __

Three
T__ __ __ __

Ten
T__ __

Five
F__ __ __ __

Eight
E__ __ __ __ __

Would you like cream or sugar in your coffee?
W__ __ __ __ y__ __ l__ __ __ cream __ __ Sugar __ __ __ __ __ __ Coffee?

Rocks • Rocks • R__ __ __ __ __ • Sand • Sand • S__ __ __ • Water

Nature Study

Go outside and make a realistic drawing of something you find in in nature.

Reading Time

Read a few pages from four books in your stack.

Copy something from each book.

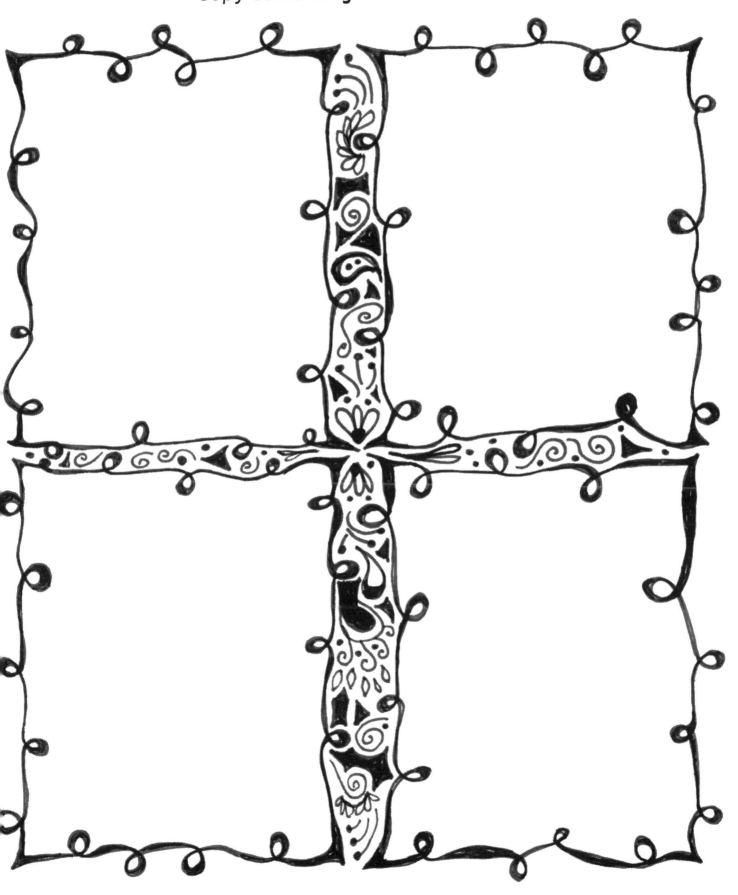

Spelling Time

Find 20 Words with 8 letters each.

Write the words here:

_____   _____

_____   _____

_____   _____

_____   _____

_____   _____

_____   _____

_____   _____

_____   _____

_____   _____

_____   _____

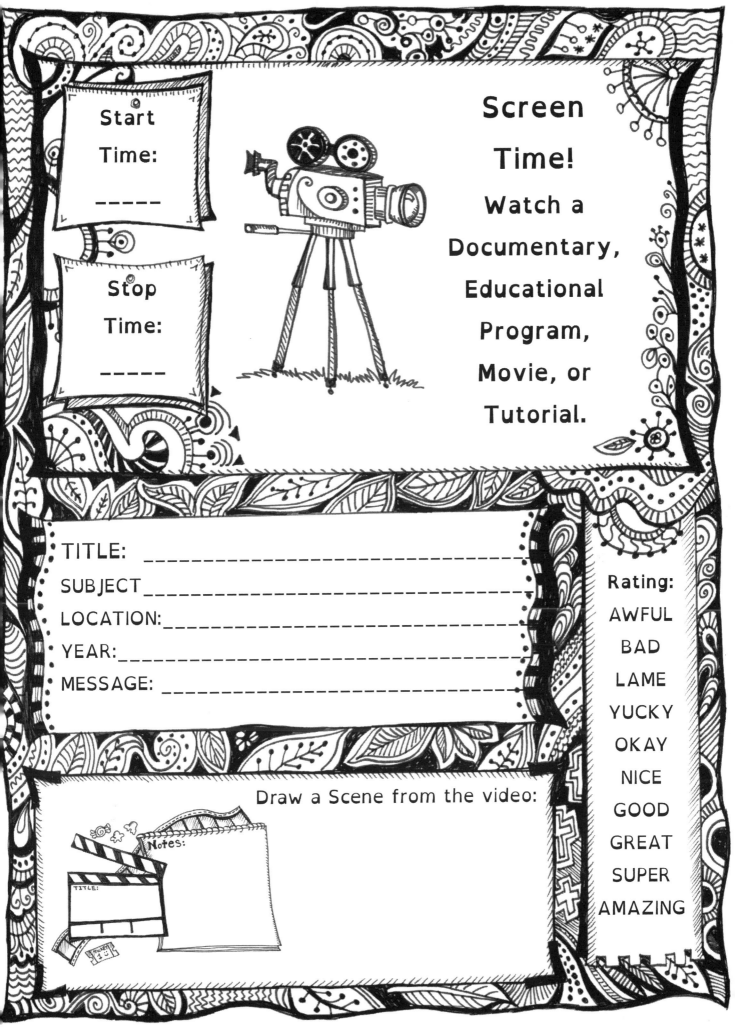

Start Time:

_ _ _ _ _

Stop Time:

_ _ _ _ _

Screen Time!

Watch a Documentary, Educational Program, Movie, or Tutorial.

TITLE: _____

SUBJECT _____

LOCATION: _____

YEAR: _____

MESSAGE: _____

Rating:
AWFUL
BAD
LAME
YUCKY
OKAY
NICE
GOOD
GREAT
SUPER
AMAZING

Draw a Scene from the video:

Notes:

TITLE:

Writing Time

Stories, Poems, Lists and More.

That's what this page is waiting for!

_____

_____

_____

_____

_____

_____

_____

_____

_____

_____

_____

_____

_____

_____

_____

_____

_____

Circle Today's Date

January
February
March
April
May
June
July
August
September
October
November
December

1 2 3 4 5 6
7 8 9 10 11
12 13 14 15
16 17 18 19
20 21 22 23
24 25 26 27
28 29 30 31

MONDAY
TUESDAY
WEDNESDAY
THURSDAY
FRIDAY
SATURDAY
SUNDAY

2015
2016
2017
2018
2019
2020
2021
2023
2024
2025
2026
2027
2028
2029
2030

Write Today's Date:_____

Start Your Day!

Inspirational Verse or Quote

_____

_____

_____

_____

_____

_____

_____

Prayer Needs

_____

_____

_____

To-Do List

_____

_____

_____

_____

_____

Art & Logic Games

Nature Study

Go outside and make a realistic
drawing of something you find in
in nature.

Reading Time

Read a few pages from four books in your stack.

Copy something from each book.

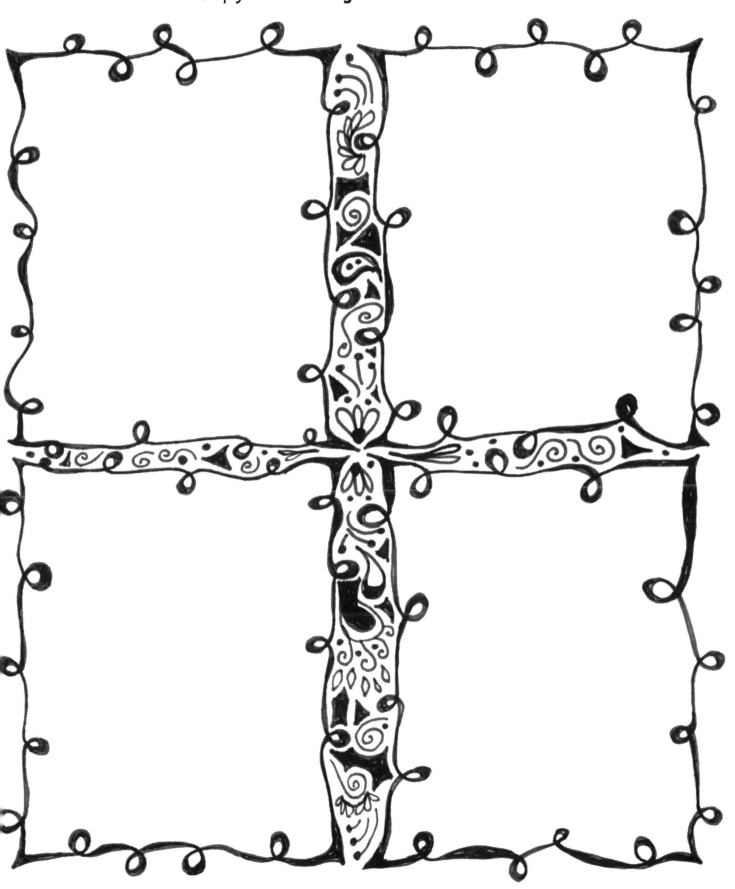

Spelling Time

Find 20 Words with 7 letters each.
Write the words here:

Screen Time!

Start Time:

_ _ _ _ _

Stop Time:

_ _ _ _ _

Watch a Documentary, Educational Program, Movie, or Tutorial.

TITLE: _____

SUBJECT _____

LOCATION: _____

YEAR: _____

MESSAGE: _____

Rating:

AWFUL

BAD

LAME

YUCKY

OKAY

NICE

GOOD

GREAT

SUPER

AMAZING

Draw a Scene from the video:

Notes:

TITLE:

DRAW THE PAST, PRESENT & FUTURE

Of _____

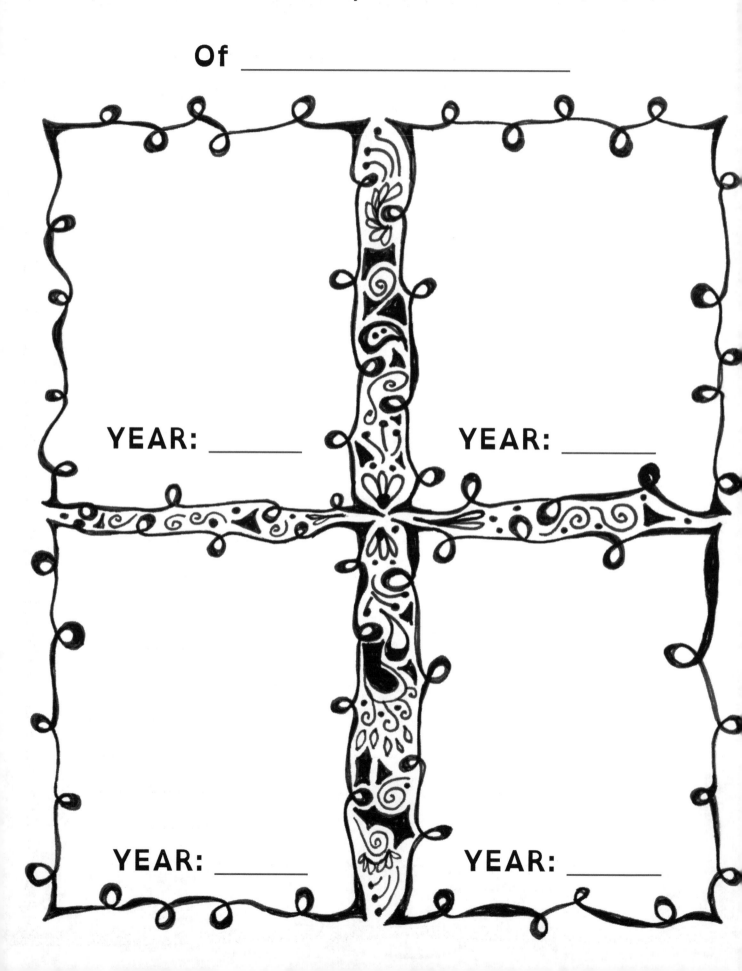

YEAR: _____

YEAR: _____

YEAR: _____

YEAR: _____

Writing Time

Stories, Poems, Lists and More.

That's what this page is waiting for!

_____

_____

_____

_____

_____

_____

_____

_____

_____

_____

_____

_____

_____

_____

_____

_____

_____

_____

Circle Today's Date

January
February
March
April
May
June
July
August
September
October
November
December

1 2 3 4 5 6
7 8 9 10 11
12 13 14 15
16 17 18 19
20 21 22 23
24 25 26 27
28 29 30 31

MONDAY
TUESDAY
WEDNESDAY
THURSDAY
FRIDAY
SATURDAY
SUNDAY

2015
2016
2017
2018
2019
2020
2021
2023
2024
2025
2026
2027
2028
2029
2030

Write Today's Date:_____

Start Your Day!

Inspirational Verse or Quote

_____

_____

_____

_____

_____

_____

Prayer Needs

_____

_____

_____

To-Do List

_____

_____

_____

_____

_____

Art & Logic Games

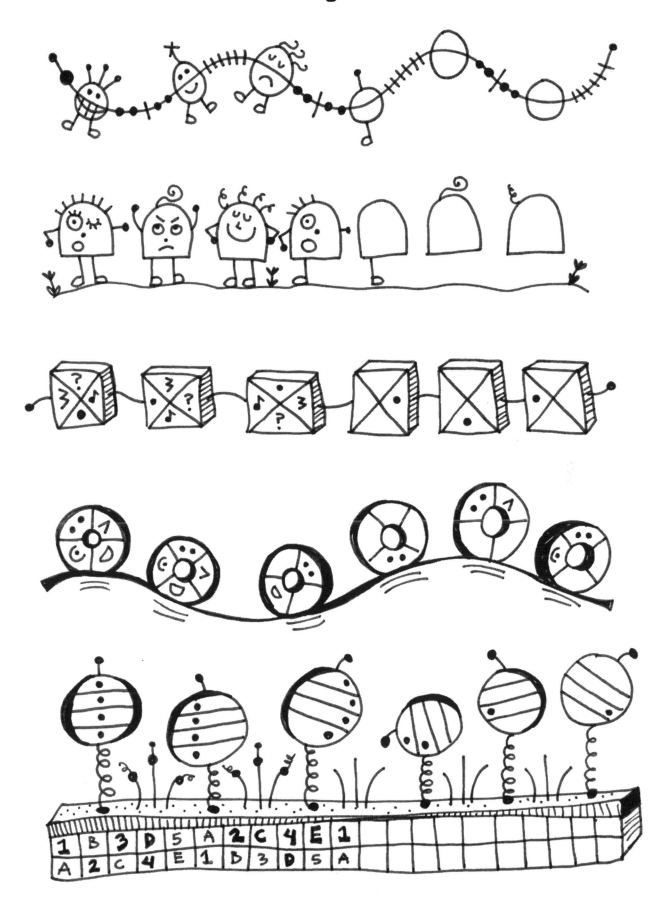

Nature Study

Go outside and make a realistic drawing of something you find in in nature.

Screen Time!

Watch a Documentary, Educational Program, Movie, or Tutorial.

Start Time:

Stop Time:

TITLE: _____

SUBJECT _____

LOCATION: _____

YEAR: _____

MESSAGE: _____

Rating:

AWFUL

BAD

LAME

YUCKY

OKAY

NICE

GOOD

GREAT

SUPER

AMAZING

Draw a Scene from the video:

Notes:

TITLE:

Writing Time

Stories, Poems, Lists and More.
That's what this page is waiting for!

_____

_____

_____

_____

_____

_____

_____

_____

_____

_____

_____

_____

_____

_____

_____

_____

_____

_____

_____

_____

Circle Today's Date

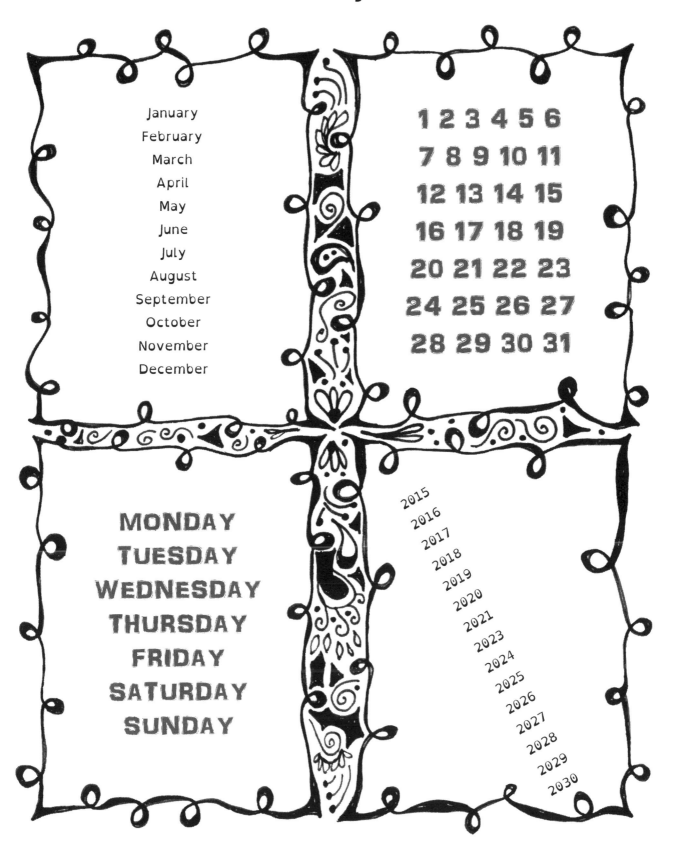

January
February
March
April
May
June
July
August
September
October
November
December

1 2 3 4 5 6
7 8 9 10 11
12 13 14 15
16 17 18 19
20 21 22 23
24 25 26 27
28 29 30 31

MONDAY
TUESDAY
WEDNESDAY
THURSDAY
FRIDAY
SATURDAY
SUNDAY

2015
2016
2017
2018
2019
2020
2021
2023
2024
2025
2026
2027
2028
2029
2030

Write Today's Date:_____

Start Your Day!

Inspirational Verse or Quote

_____
_____
_____
_____
_____
_____

Prayer Needs

_____
_____
_____
_____

To-Do List

_____
_____
_____
_____
_____

Art & Logic Games

Nature Study

Go outside and make a realistic drawing of something you find in in nature.

Reading Time

Read a few pages from four books in your stack.

Copy something from each book.

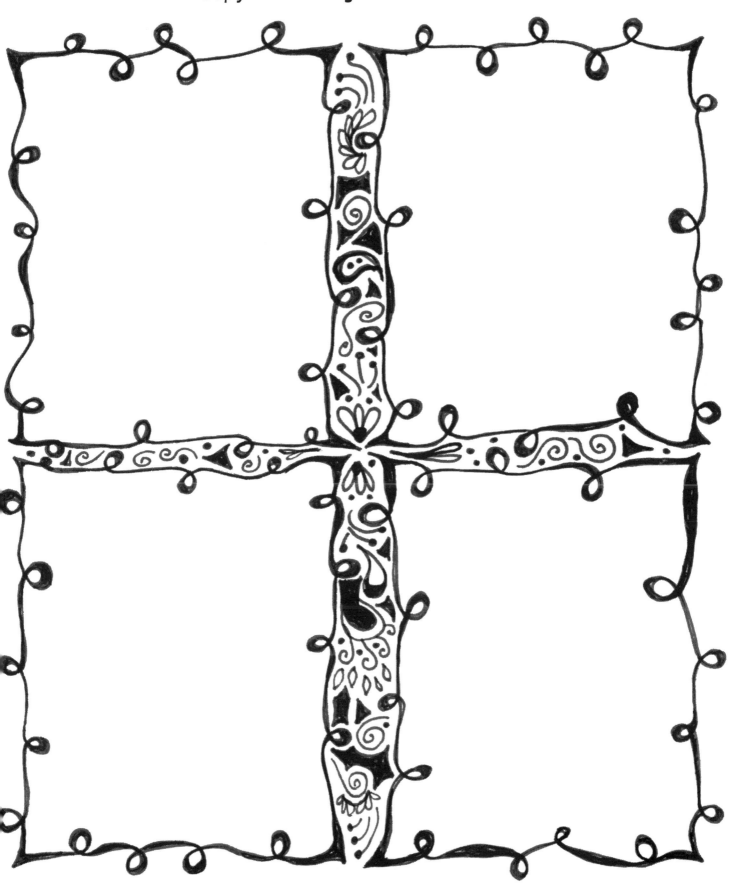

Spelling Time

Find 20 Words with 5 letters each.

Write the words here:

_____   _____

_____   _____

_____   _____

_____   _____

_____   _____

_____   _____

_____   _____

_____   _____

_____   _____

_____   _____

Start Time:

_ _ _ _ _

Stop Time:

_ _ _ _ _

Screen Time!

Watch a Documentary, Educational Program, Movie, or Tutorial.

TITLE: _____

SUBJECT _____

LOCATION: _____

YEAR: _____

MESSAGE: _____

Rating:

AWFUL

BAD

LAME

YUCKY

OKAY

NICE

GOOD

GREAT

SUPER

AMAZING

Draw a Scene from the video:

Notes:

TITLE:

World News Today!

What do you think is the most important thing that happened in the world today?

Tell the story with words or pictures.

Writing Time

Stories, Poems, Lists and More.

That's what this page is waiting for!

_____

_____

_____

_____

_____

_____

_____

_____

_____

_____

_____

_____

_____

_____

_____

_____

_____

_____

_____

_____

Circle Today's Date

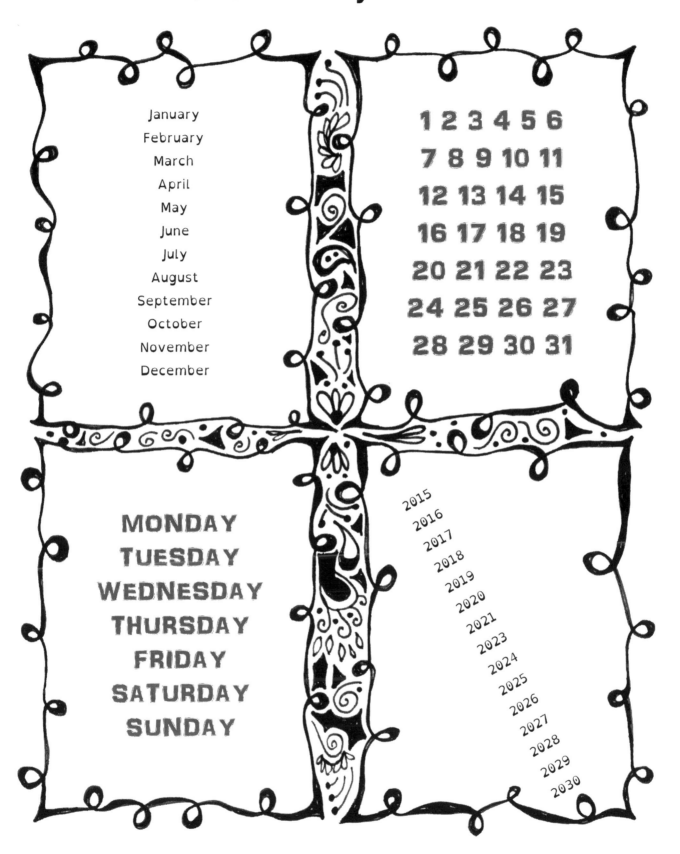

January
February
March
April
May
June
July
August
September
October
November
December

1 2 3 4 5 6
7 8 9 10 11
12 13 14 15
16 17 18 19
20 21 22 23
24 25 26 27
28 29 30 31

MONDAY
TUESDAY
WEDNESDAY
THURSDAY
FRIDAY
SATURDAY
SUNDAY

2015
2016
2017
2018
2019
2020
2021
2023
2024
2025
2026
2027
2028
2029
2030

Write Today's Date:_____

Start Your Day!

Inspirational Verse or Quote

_____

_____

_____

_____

_____

_____

Prayer Needs

_____

_____

_____

_____

To-Do List

_____

_____

_____

_____

_____

Art & Logic Games

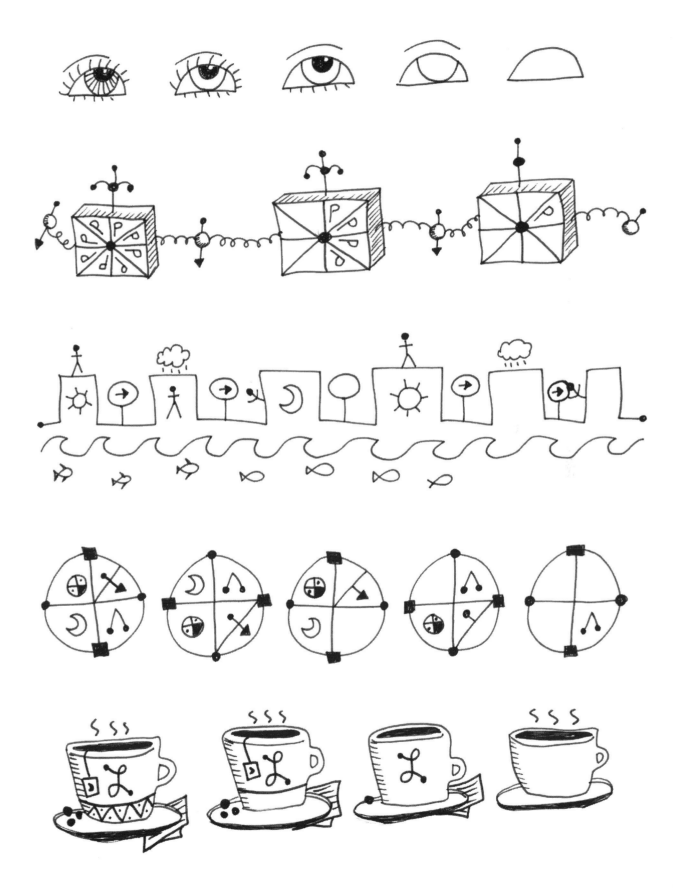

Nature Study

Go outside and make a realistic drawing of something you find in in nature.

Reading Time

Read a few pages from four books in your stack.

Copy something from each book.

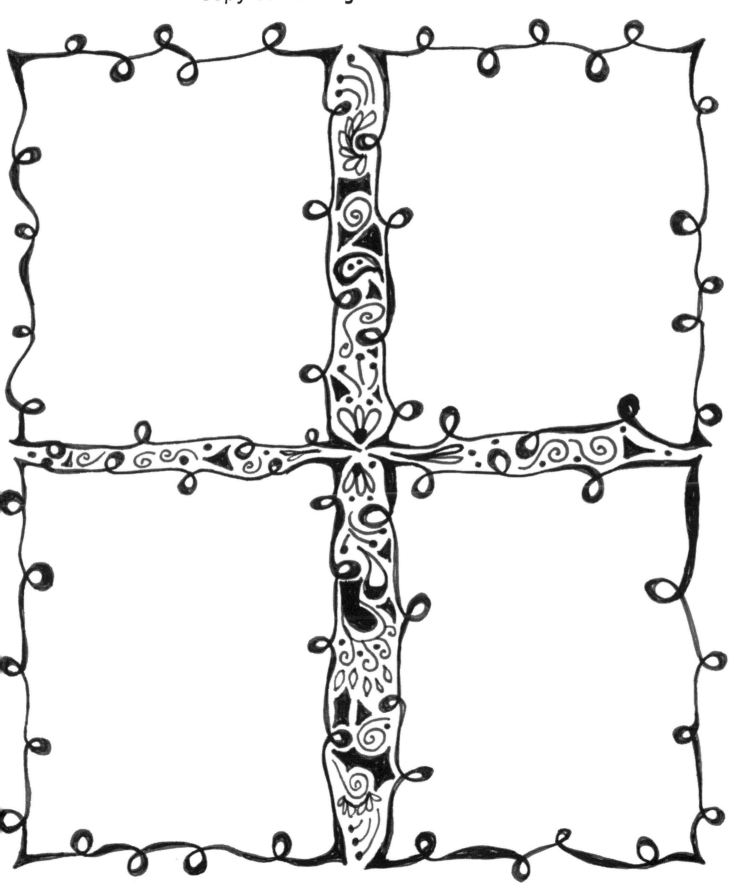

Spelling Time

Find 20 Words with 6 letters each.
Write the words here:

_____   _____

_____   _____

_____   _____

_____   _____

_____   _____

_____   _____

_____   _____

_____   _____

_____   _____

_____   _____

Screen Time!

Start Time:

Stop Time:

Watch a Documentary, Educational Program, Movie, or Tutorial.

TITLE: _____

SUBJECT _____

LOCATION: _____

YEAR: _____

MESSAGE: _____

Rating:
AWFUL
BAD
LAME
YUCKY
OKAY
NICE
GOOD
GREAT
SUPER
AMAZING

Draw a Scene from the video:

Notes:

TITLE:

Listening Time

Listen to an audio book or classical music or
ask someone to read a story to you while
you color and draw on the next page.

What are you listening to?

_____

Circle Today's Date

January
February
March
April
May
June
July
August
September
October
November
December

1 2 3 4 5 6
7 8 9 10 11
12 13 14 15
16 17 18 19
20 21 22 23
24 25 26 27
28 29 30 31

MONDAY
TUESDAY
WEDNESDAY
THURSDAY
FRIDAY
SATURDAY
SUNDAY

2015
2016
2017
2018
2019
2020
2021
2023
2024
2025
2026
2027
2028
2029
2030

Write Today's Date:_____

Start Your Day!

Inspirational Verse or Quote

_____

_____

_____

_____

_____

_____

Prayer Needs

_____

_____

_____

_____

To-Do List

_____

_____

_____

_____

_____

Art & Logic Games

Nature Study

Go outside and make a realistic drawing of something you find in in nature.

Reading Time

Read a few pages from four books in your stack.
Copy something from each book.

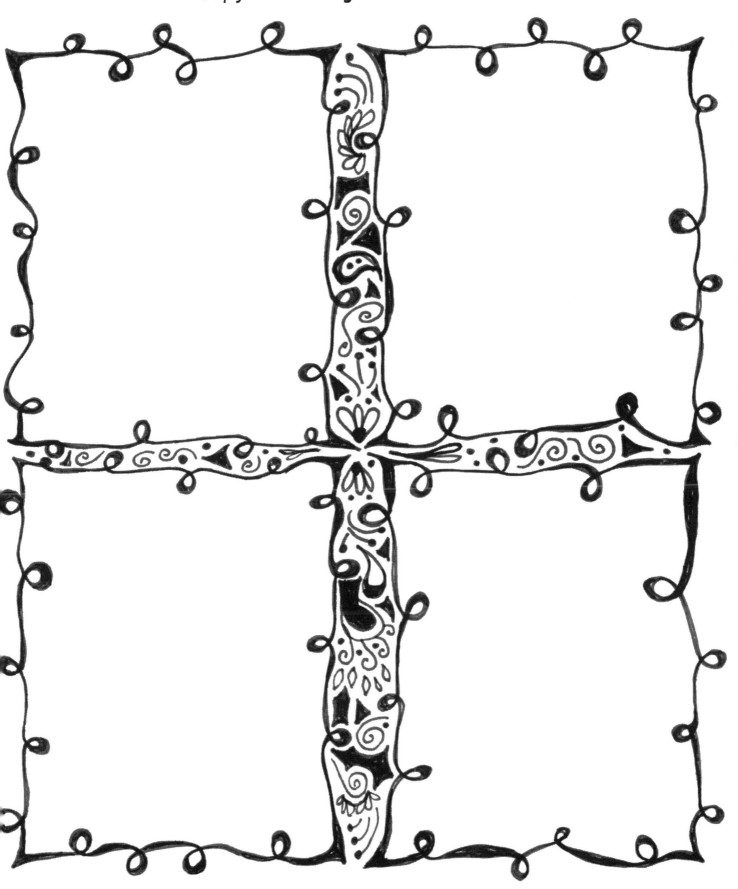

Spelling Time

Find 20 Words with **7** letters each.
Write the words here:

_____   _____

_____   _____

_____   _____

_____   _____

_____   _____

_____   _____

_____   _____

_____   _____

_____   _____

_____   _____

Start Time:

_ _ _ _ _

Stop Time:

_ _ _ _ _

Screen Time!

Watch a Documentary, Educational Program, Movie, or Tutorial.

TITLE: _____

SUBJECT _____

LOCATION:_____

YEAR:_____

MESSAGE: _____

Rating:

AWFUL

BAD

LAME

YUCKY

OKAY

NICE

GOOD

GREAT

SUPER

AMAZING

Draw a Scene from the video:

Notes:

TITLE:

DRAW THE PAST, PRESENT & FUTURE

Of _____

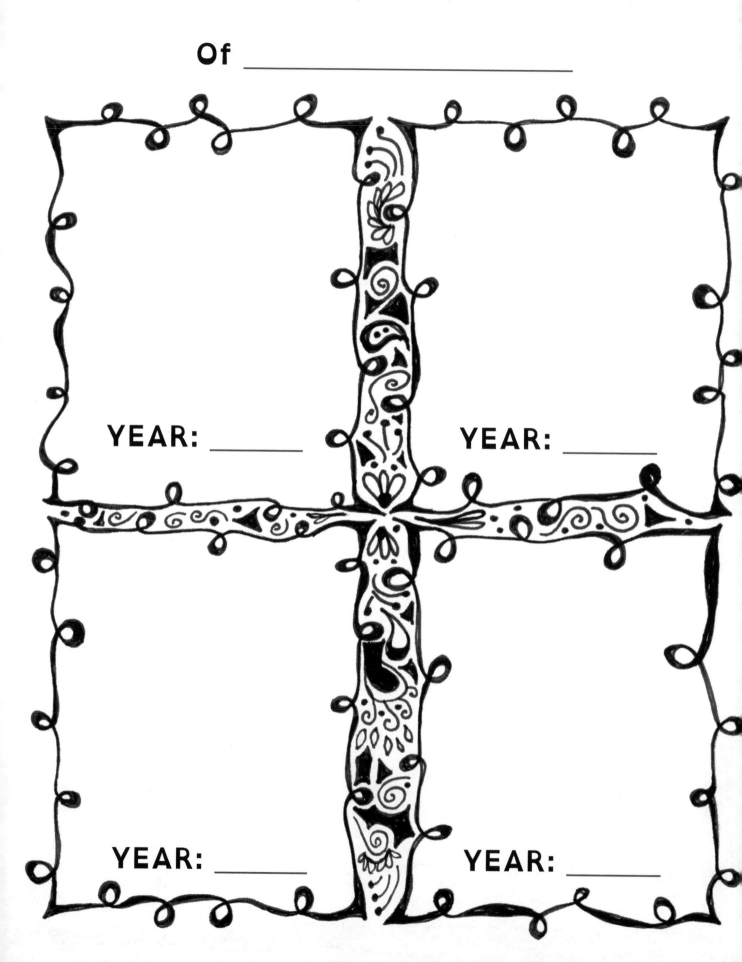

YEAR: _____

YEAR: _____

YEAR: _____

YEAR: _____

Writing Time

Stories, Poems, Lists and More.

That's what this page is waiting for!

Circle Today's Date

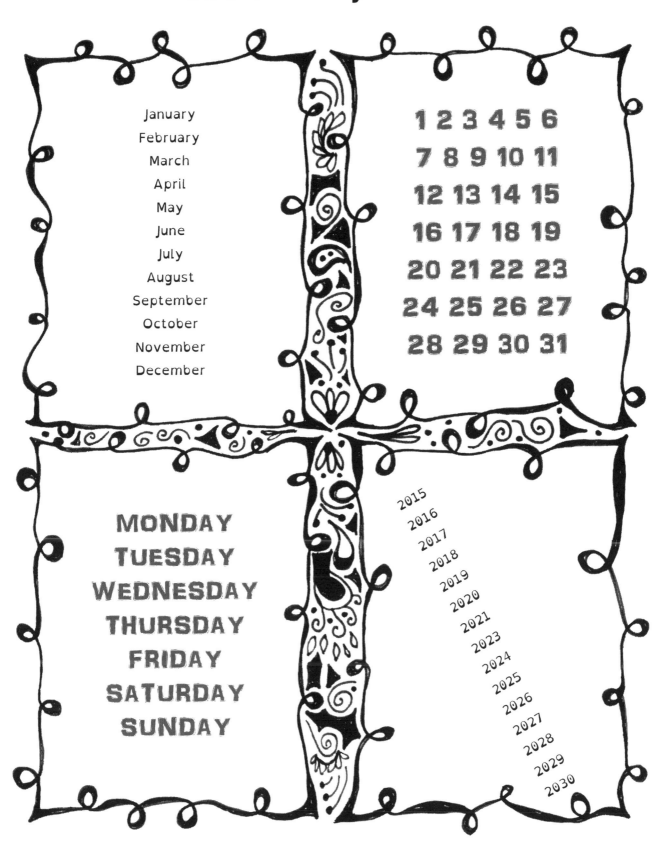

January
February
March
April
May
June
July
August
September
October
November
December

1 2 3 4 5 6
7 8 9 10 11
12 13 14 15
16 17 18 19
20 21 22 23
24 25 26 27
28 29 30 31

MONDAY
TUESDAY
WEDNESDAY
THURSDAY
FRIDAY
SATURDAY
SUNDAY

2015
2016
2017
2018
2019
2020
2021
2023
2024
2025
2026
2027
2028
2029
2030

Write Today's Date:_____

Start Your Day!

Inspirational Verse or Quote

_____

_____

_____

_____

_____

_____

Prayer Needs

_____

_____

_____

_____

To-Do List

_____

_____

_____

_____

_____

Art & Logic Games

Nature Study

Go outside and make a realistic
drawing of something you find in
in nature.

Reading Time

Read a few pages from four books in your stack.

Copy something from each book.

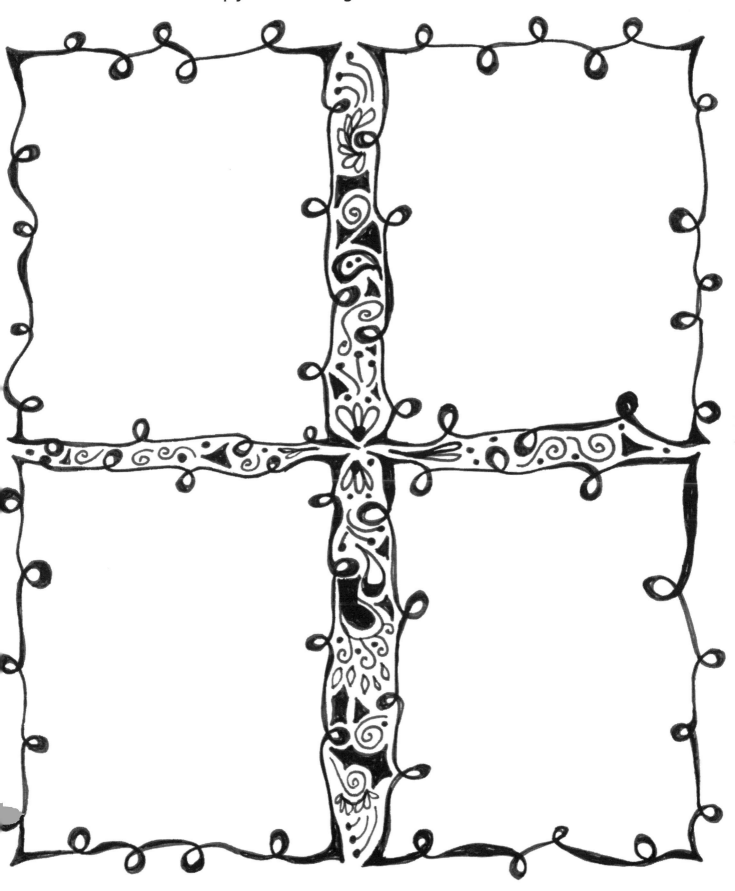

Spelling Time

Find 20 Words with 8 letters each.

Write the words here:

_____   _____

_____   _____

_____   _____

_____   _____

_____   _____

_____   _____

_____   _____

_____   _____

_____   _____

_____   _____

Start Time: _____

Stop Time: _____

Screen Time!

Watch a Documentary, Educational Program, Movie, or Tutorial.

TITLE: _____

SUBJECT _____

LOCATION: _____

YEAR: _____

MESSAGE: _____

Rating:

AWFUL

BAD

LAME

YUCKY

OKAY

NICE

GOOD

GREAT

SUPER

AMAZING

Draw a Scene from the video:

Notes:

TITLE:

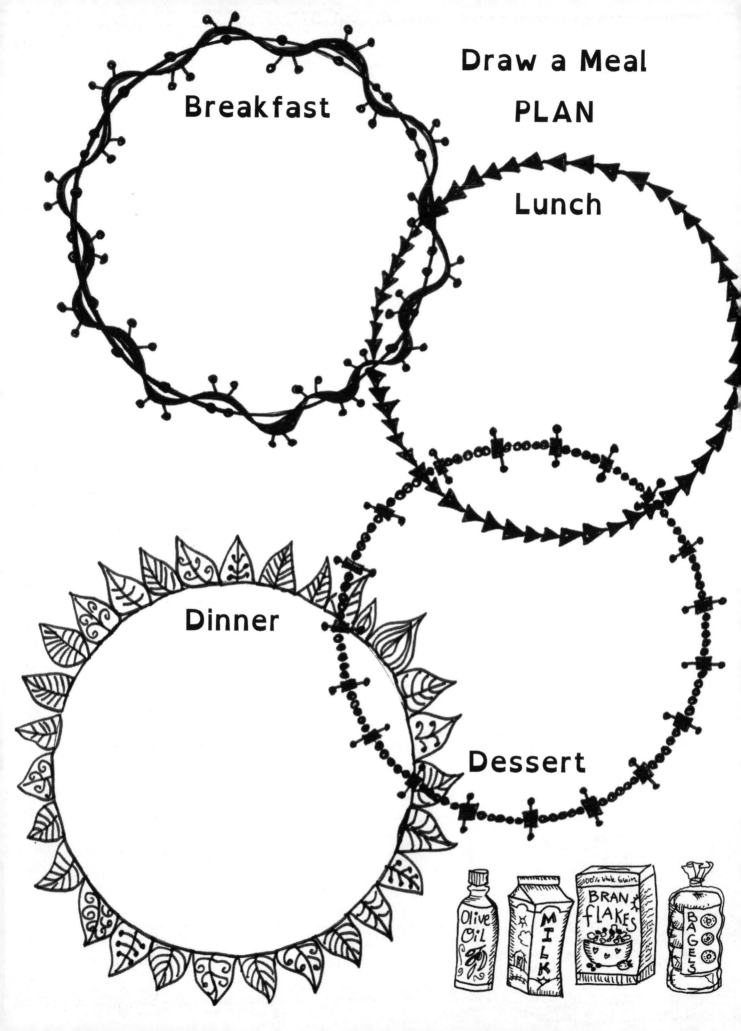

Writing Time

Stories, Poems, Lists and More.

That's what this page is waiting for!

_____

_____

_____

_____

_____

_____

_____

_____

_____

_____

_____

_____

_____

_____

_____

_____

_____

Circle Today's Date

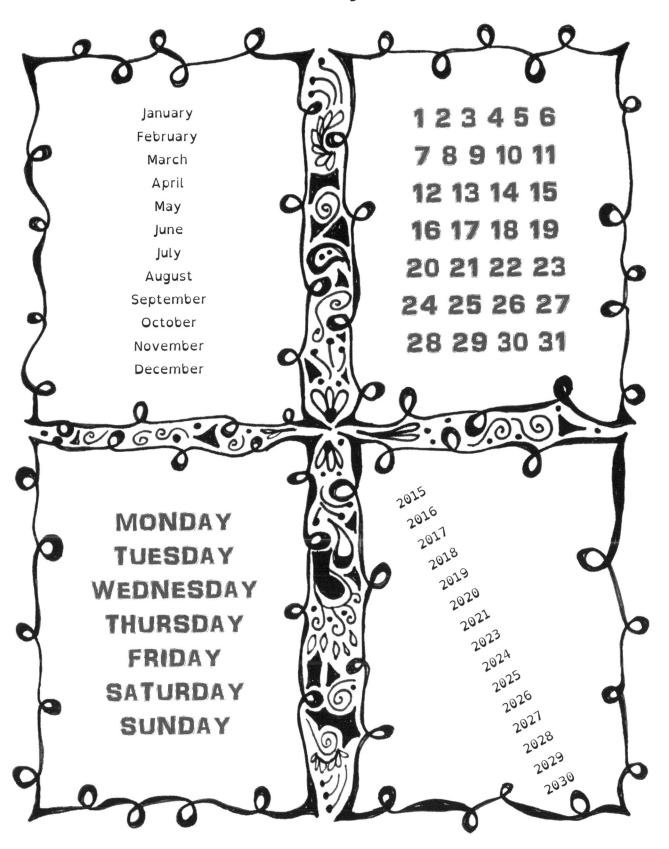

January
February
March
April
May
June
July
August
September
October
November
December

1 2 3 4 5 6
7 8 9 10 11
12 13 14 15
16 17 18 19
20 21 22 23
24 25 26 27
28 29 30 31

MONDAY
TUESDAY
WEDNESDAY
THURSDAY
FRIDAY
SATURDAY
SUNDAY

2015
2016
2017
2018
2019
2020
2021
2023
2024
2025
2026
2027
2028
2029
2030

Write Today's Date:_____

Start Your Day!

Inspirational Verse or Quote

_____

_____

_____

_____

_____

_____

Prayer Needs

_____

_____

_____

To-Do List

_____

_____

_____

_____

_____

Art & Logic Games

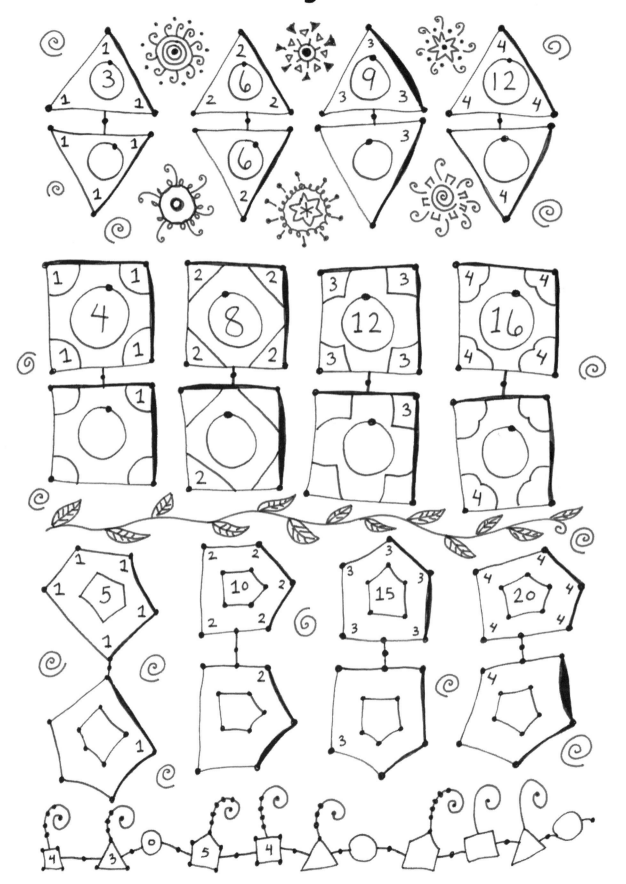

Nature Study

Go outside and make a realistic drawing of something you find in in nature.

Reading Time

Read a few pages from four books in your stack.
Copy something from each book.

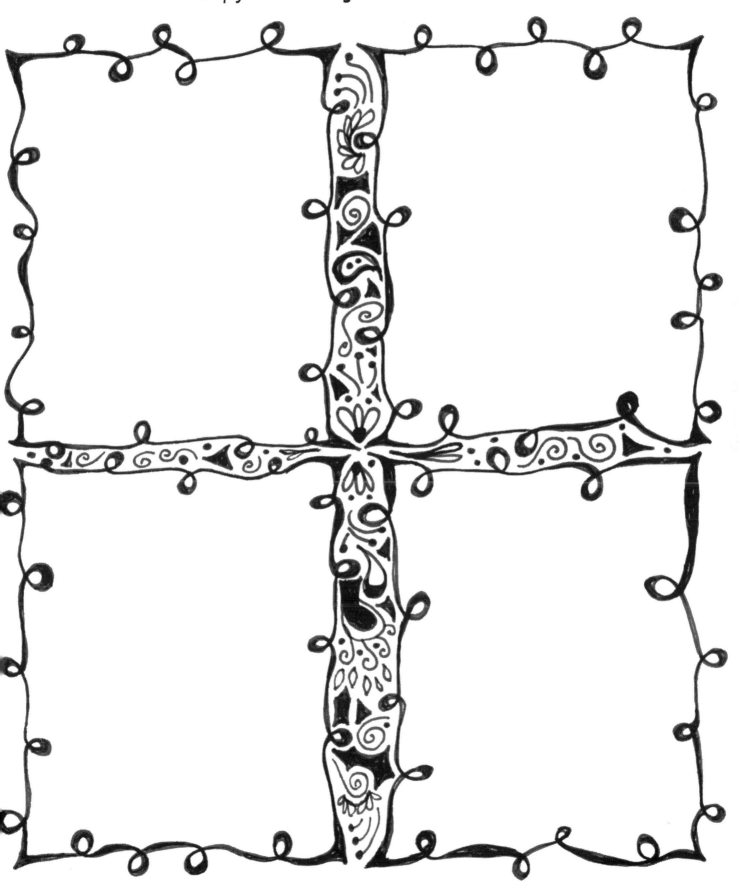

Spelling Time

Find 20 Words with 7 letters each.

Write the words here:

_____   _____

_____   _____

_____   _____

_____   _____

_____   _____

_____   _____

_____   _____

_____   _____

_____   _____

_____   _____

Screen Time!

Watch a Documentary, Educational Program, Movie, or Tutorial.

Start Time: _ _ _ _ _

Stop Time: _ _ _ _ _

TITLE: _____

SUBJECT _____

LOCATION: _____

YEAR: _____

MESSAGE: _____

Rating:

AWFUL

BAD

LAME

YUCKY

OKAY

NICE

GOOD

GREAT

SUPER

AMAZING

Draw a Scene from the video:

Notes:

TITLE:

Writing Time

Stories, Poems, Lists and More.
That's what this page is waiting for!

_____

_____

_____

_____

_____

_____

_____

_____

_____

_____

_____

_____

_____

_____

_____

_____

_____

_____

Circle Today's Date

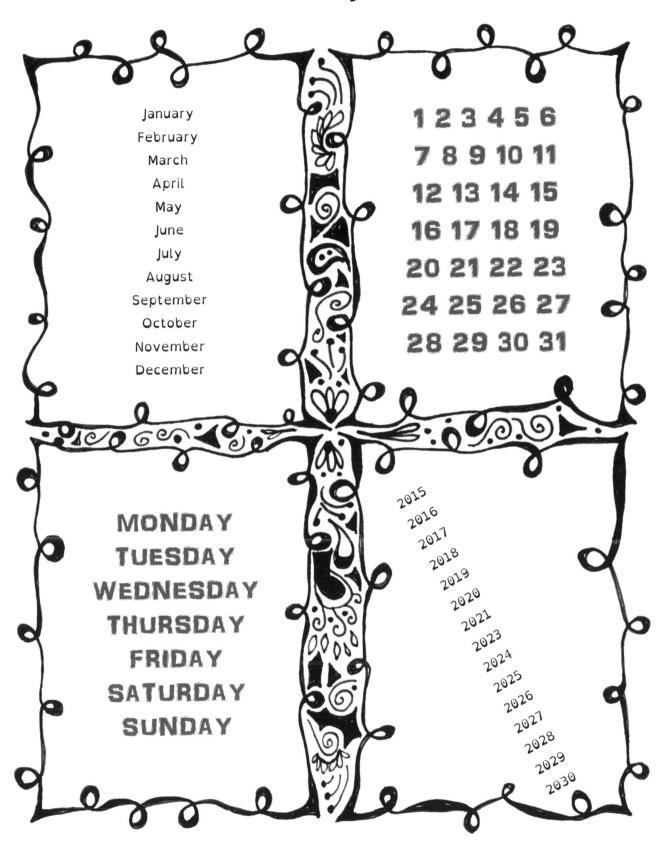

January
February
March
April
May
June
July
August
September
October
November
December

1 2 3 4 5 6
7 8 9 10 11
12 13 14 15
16 17 18 19
20 21 22 23
24 25 26 27
28 29 30 31

MONDAY
TUESDAY
WEDNESDAY
THURSDAY
FRIDAY
SATURDAY
SUNDAY

2015
2016
2017
2018
2019
2020
2021
2023
2024
2025
2026
2027
2028
2029
2030

Write Today's Date:_____

Start Your Day!

Inspirational Verse or Quote

_____

_____

_____

_____

_____

_____

Prayer Needs

_____

_____

_____

_____

To-Do List

_____

_____

_____

_____

_____

Art & Logic Games

Nature Study

Go outside and make a realistic
drawing of something you find in
in nature.

Reading Time

Read a few pages from four books in your stack.
Copy something from each book.

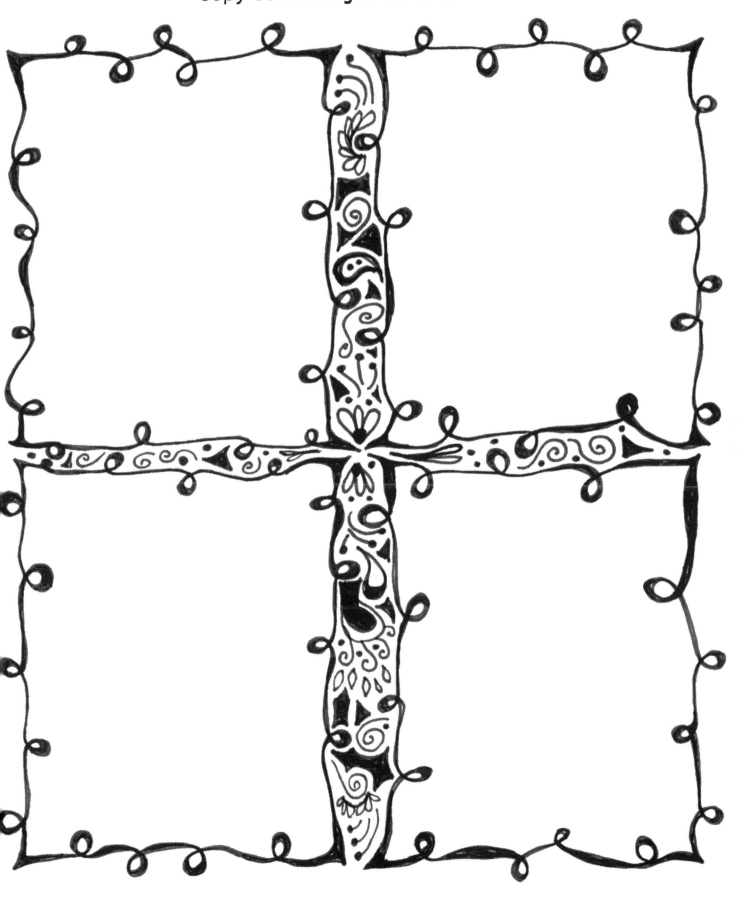

Spelling Time

Find 20 Words with 7 letters each.

Write the words here:

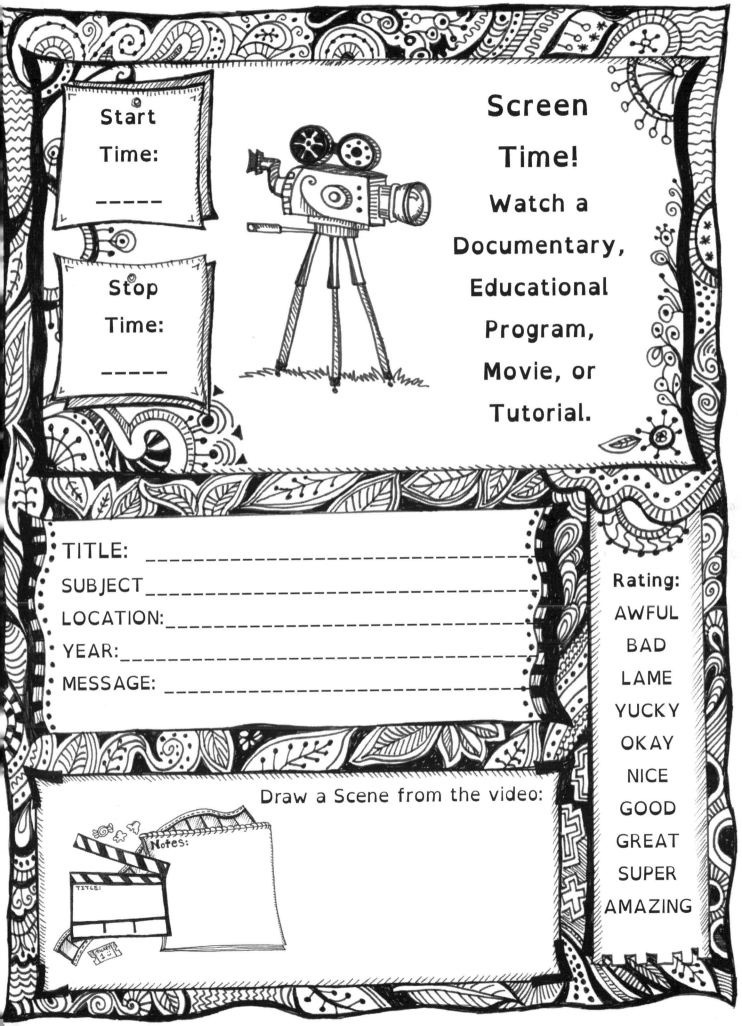

Start Time:
_ _ _ _ _

Stop Time:
_ _ _ _ _

Screen Time!

Watch a Documentary, Educational Program, Movie, or Tutorial.

TITLE: _____

SUBJECT _____

LOCATION: _____

YEAR: _____

MESSAGE: _____

Rating:

AWFUL

BAD

LAME

YUCKY

OKAY

NICE

GOOD

GREAT

SUPER

AMAZING

Draw a Scene from the video:

Notes:

TITLE:

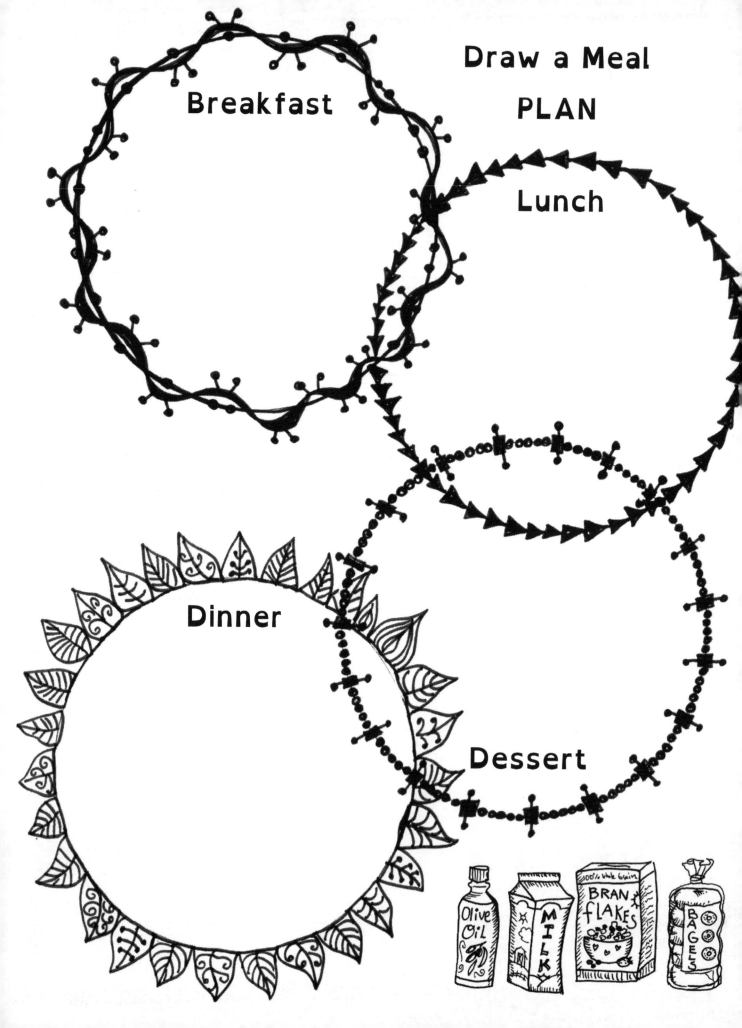

Breakfast

Draw a Meal
PLAN

Lunch

Dinner

Dessert

Writing Time

Stories, Poems, Lists and More.
That's what this page is waiting for!

_____

_____

_____

_____

_____

_____

_____

_____

_____

_____

_____

_____

_____

_____

_____

_____

_____

_____

Circle Today's Date

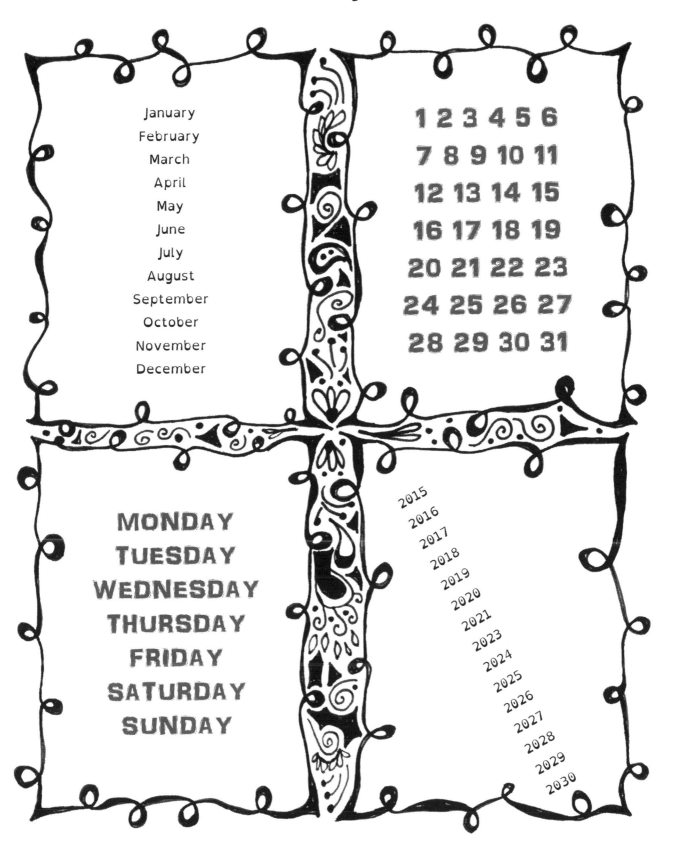

January
February
March
April
May
June
July
August
September
October
November
December

1 2 3 4 5 6
7 8 9 10 11
12 13 14 15
16 17 18 19
20 21 22 23
24 25 26 27
28 29 30 31

MONDAY
TUESDAY
WEDNESDAY
THURSDAY
FRIDAY
SATURDAY
SUNDAY

2015
2016
2017
2018
2019
2020
2021
2023
2024
2025
2026
2027
2028
2029
2030

Write Today's Date:_____

Start Your Day!

Inspirational Verse or Quote

_____

_____

_____

_____

_____

_____

Prayer Needs

_____

_____

_____

_____

To-Do List

_____

_____

_____

_____

_____

Art & Logic Games

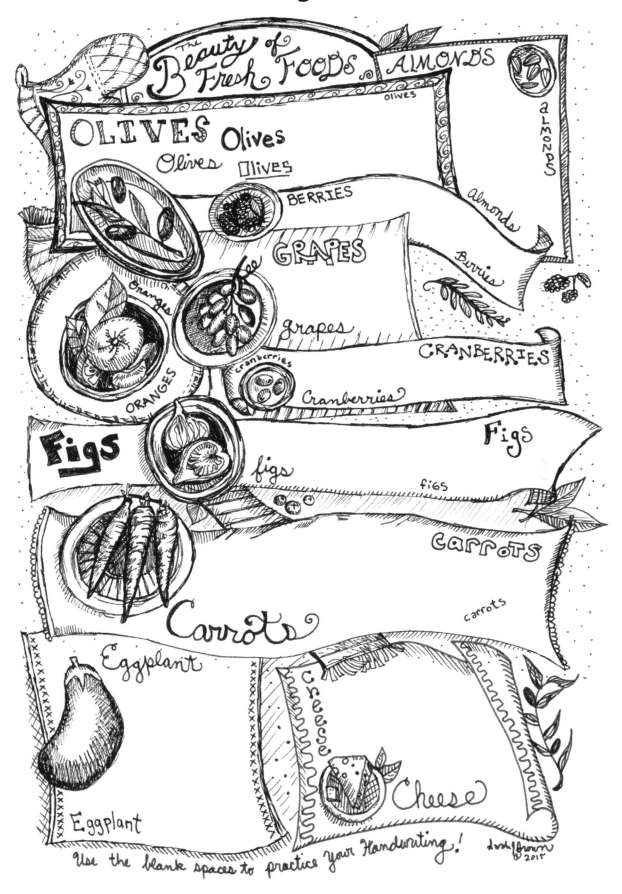

The Beauty of Fresh Foods

ALMONDS

OLIVES Olives Olives Olives

olives

ALMONDS

BERRIES

GRAPES

Almonds

Oranges

grapes

Berries

ORANGES

cranberries

CRANBERRIES

Cranberries

Figs

Figs

figs

figs

ORANGES

Carrots

carrots

Carrots

Eggplant

Cheese

Eggplant

Cheese

Use the blank spaces to practice your Handwriting!

Nature Study

Go outside and make a realistic drawing of something you find in in nature.

Reading Time

Read a few pages from four books in your stack.
Copy something from each book.

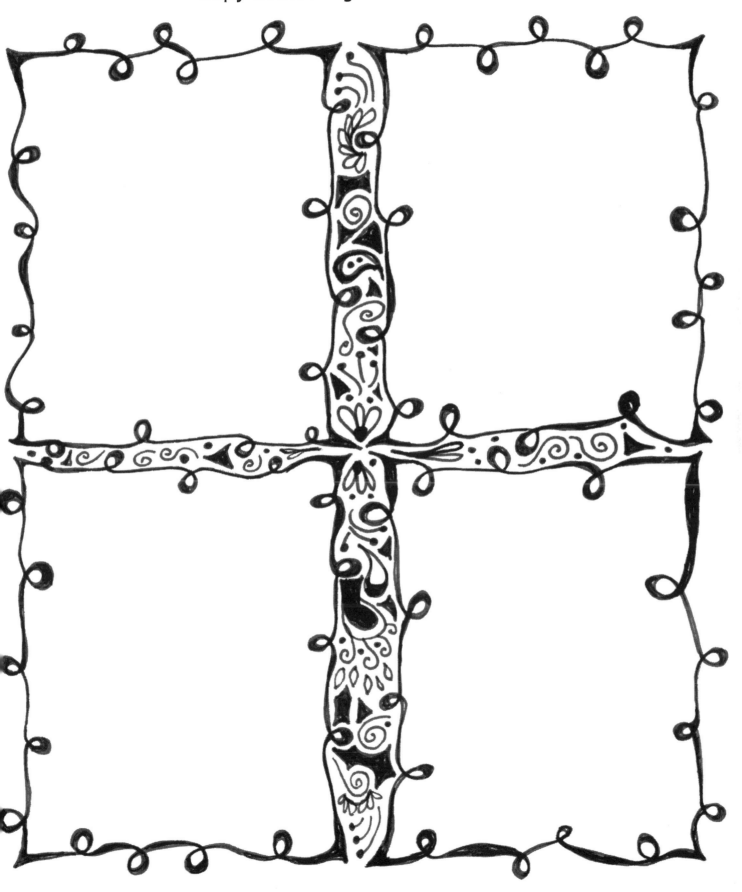

Spelling Time

Find 20 Words with 10 letters each.
Write the words here:

Start Time:

_ _ _ _ _

Stop Time:

_ _ _ _ _

Screen Time!

Watch a Documentary, Educational Program, Movie, or Tutorial.

TITLE: _____

SUBJECT _____

LOCATION: _____

YEAR: _____

MESSAGE: _____

Rating:

AWFUL

BAD

LAME

YUCKY

OKAY

NICE

GOOD

GREAT

SUPER

AMAZING

Notes:

TITLE:

Draw a Scene from the video:

Writing Time

Stories, Poems, Lists and More.

That's what this page is waiting for!

_____

_____

_____

_____

_____

_____

_____

_____

_____

_____

_____

_____

_____

_____

_____

_____

_____

_____

_____

21236267R00174

Made in the USA
Middletown, DE
27 June 2015